Wakefield Press

KIERAN MODRA

Andy Thurlow is a retired primary school teacher, having taught in both private and government schools throughout Australia. Born in the Channel Islands, he now lives in the Barossa Valley in South Australia. He is married with two children.

[Photo: Theo Modra]

Praise for *Kieran Modra: The Way I See It*

The words 'role model' are often used but rarely are they done justice. With Kieran Modra you have a genuine, authentic Aussie hero whose attitude we all should aspire to. If we need inspiration he should be the benchmark. – Steve Waugh, former Australian cricketer

Kieran is a talented sportsman and an outstanding South Australian. His passion, vision and resilience are an inspiration to us all. – His Excellency the Honourable Hieu Van Le AC, Governor of South Australia

This is the story of one of South Australia's under-the-radar sporting stars. Kieran blazed a trail for many in the Paralympic movement, including myself. His story demonstrates what can be achieved with a positive attitude and a huge amount of hard work. I thoroughly enjoyed this book. – Matt Cowdrey, winner of 13 Paralympic gold medals

It's a wonderful story and shows the courage of a young man, who has already achieved so much in such a short time. Kieran is a trailblazer for all disabled athletes to look up to for inspiration. – Dawn Fraser, AO, MBE

Andy Thurlow has masterfully pulled together a remarkable insight into Kieran's life. A 'must read' for all ages. – Murray Lydeamore, former Australian Paralympic Cycling Team Manager

A great read. Follow Kieran as he faces his challenges and with ability, overcomes adversity. Kieran is one of the most physical, naturally gifted athletes I have been lucky to work with. – Peter Day, Head Coach, Cycling Australia

Kieran has helped pave the way for athletes and people with a disability. He is ferociously determined and yet caring, sensitive and always likes a laugh. This is a book that all should read to better understand the power of the human spirit. – Kurt Fearnley, three-time Paralympic gold medalist

KIERAN MODRA

THE WAY I SEE IT

as told to

ANDY THURLOW

Wakefield Press

Wakefield Press
16 Rose Street
Mile End
South Australia 5031
wakefieldpress.com.au

First published 2018
This edition published 2019

Edited by Julia Beaven, Wakefield Press
Typeset by Michael Deves, Wakefield Press

ISBN 978 1 74305 699 8

A catalogue record for this book is available from the National Library of Australia

For my dad, Stanley Victor Thurlow (1914–1974)

and

Darren Theodore Modra (1967–2016)

and my living treasures
Marley, Daniel, Lauren and Mum

Contents

Author's Note

Some stories need to be told. Kieran is my wife Marlene's nephew, so I have watched him grow up. I first wrote Kieran's story like a narrator in a play, quoting him in italics. Authors are probably their own harshest critics and I was happier when, after consulting Kieran, I converted the story to first person. Well, most of it. At times, I needed to be an *italicised narrator.* I trust that by climbing into Kieran's large shoes (when he wears them), I help to involve and absorb you more fully. As with any oral history there may be minor inaccuracies, but I have endeavoured to be open, honest and transparent. We both have. I think Kieran is an exceptional human being, but not perfect. Above all, Kieran is modest. If, in this book, he comes across to you in any way arrogant or self-absorbed, that is the fault of the writer. The nice thing about a book is you can have your own opinion.

Prologue

It was December and I was riding my bike in heavy morning traffic. I didn't see the parked car. My head hit and dented the top of the car and my hand went through the back window. I was flung on to the road and was fortunate not to have been run over by following traffic. The hatchback I hit was a write-off.

The surgeons were worried the broken tip of my C3 neck vertebra might float around and do further damage. More dangerous still was a compound fracture to the L4 vertebra in my lower back. Transferred to Flinders Medical Centre, I was kept in a brace and was not allowed to move for ten days.

Kerry remembers:

> Kieran was having memory issues and the neurologist asked me to bring in his helmet – the outer shell appeared almost perfect, but the foam was full of hairline cracks. Kieran kept begging my dad to take a photo of his bloodied face. I can't cope with blood, so I was sitting on the floor holding Kieran's hand. The doctors did a great job with his forehead. It was split almost the whole way across. He had over 160 stitches and the doctors gave it a lift at the same time. He doesn't have as many wrinkles now ...

An old friend, Jenny Flood, was shocked at Kieran's condition:

> I visited Kieran at Flinders on the fourth day after the accident. He was a real mess, and I thought nobody could get out of this. It was scary to see him like that and nobody knew if he would be able to walk again, let alone ride a bike. I had witnessed his determination and courage when he started on his journey in athletics. He was going to need all of that again just to get out of his bed.

Kieran was sore and confused. He couldn't move. He couldn't see. His surroundings were a blur, but he was used to this. He could hear snatches of conversations and he knew from the whispers his future looked grim. Was this to be the end of his dreams? Had all his effort come to this? And the nights ... he dreaded the nights. He lay straitjacketed, recalling the chapters of his life so far, and prayed for the dawn.

1 Port Lincoln and Weet-Bix

1972–1982

There are Keirens, Keirans, Kierens and Kierans. I belong to the latter group – Kieran John Modra, born in the pretty fishing town of Port Lincoln on the southern end of Eyre Peninsula in South Australia. People consistently misspell my name, which has sometimes led to this strange conversation:

'Are you related to Tony Modra, the footballer?'

'Yes,' I reply, 'Tony is distantly related, but we've never met.'

'Well then, are you related to the swimmer Kieren Perkins?'

My parents are of Germanic ancestry and are active churchgoers. My dad Theo is sixth generation Australian, Lutheran and with Wendish ancestry. Lutherans migrated to Australia from German lands in the 1830s after new Prussian laws were passed forbidding them to worship with freedom. On arriving in South Australia with a larger group of migrating Germans, the Wends became a minority within a minority, but soon merged with their fellow Lutherans establishing schools and churches. In many cases they continued to speak their German mother tongue until the outbreak of World War II.

My grandfather, Vic Modra, is a west coast farmer whose farm flourished, as did his family. Dad, the eldest of Vic and Dora's 11 children, left school at 15 and moved to Naracoorte in the South East of South Australia to develop a bush block. When it comes to anything mechanical, Dad is a genius. He also loves a challenge and when Thistle Island, near Port Lincoln, came on the market he purchased it, a ketch called the *Hecla* (the last wooden ketch of its kind to be used in South Australia), and a plane, which he learnt to fly. Against the odds, he established a viable sheep farm.

My mum, Sylvia (nee Schoff), was born in Walla Walla, New South Wales, and trained as a telephonist there. This became handy when my parents were courting long distance by phone (when the lines weren't busy). They first met at Lutheran Youth Assemblies organised around Australia. Things developed at the 21st birthday party of a mutual friend, and Mum was thrilled when Dad asked her to come with him to Windy Point. Adelaide people know it gives you a good view of the city by night. It is also well known that young Adelaide couples seldom take full advantage of this view, preferring the cosiness and warmth of the car and each other. Mum was disappointed to find out Dad had asked others along, so she was just one girl in a carload.

After marrying in 1965, my parents lived in a caravan on the Modra home property near Yeelanna, in the middle of the Eyre Peninsula, and commuted to their island from there.

Thistle Island is the second largest island off the South Australian coast, 18 km long and 3 km wide, with a history of numerous attempts at farming. During World War I it was a breeding farm for horses for the Australian Army. A whaling station had been established on the island in 1838, and previous attempts to turn it into a sheep farm were curtailed by coast disease (a wasting disease in sheep caused by cobalt deficiency in coastal soils).

Mum and Dad were determined to succeed at this enterprise. Dad's first problem was to prevent the island sheep from dying. By the late 1930s CSIRO scientists had discovered the role of cobalt in coast disease. Dad successfully protected the sheep by injecting them with a ground-up mixture of copper carbonate, amino acetic acid (glycine) and peanut oil. The farm income was supplemented with payment from sailors using Thistle as a natural sheltering spot for their boats. The previous owners had rolled their wool bales over the cliff and floated them on dinghies out to the boat. Dad blasted a road down the cliffside, bulldozed it level, and built a crane to sling the bales straight onto our ketch. He used two Blitz cranes to lower the D4 bulldozer onto the *Hecla* in Port Lincoln, then sailed into Snug Bay on the island and waited for low tide. When the ketch leaned over, he drove the dozer off into the water. He hadn't reckoned the tide would ebb so late into the evening and the dozer bogged in the beach sand, but with persistence he got it ashore by moonlight. My parents' resolve and perseverance in overcoming huge logistical problems proved them to be wonderful role models for us as children.

My eldest brother, Darren, was born at the local hospital in Cummins. Mark followed a few years later after our parents had bought a small property just out of Port Lincoln to service the island. This is the place I remember most from my childhood. Tania, my only sister, was born three years after me.

Dad loved working with engines and metalwork in his big shed and was soon making wonderful playground equipment for us. With him owning a small plane as well as an 18-metre ketch, I had a wonderful childhood. As kids, we were allowed and encouraged to try things out. My parents adopted a philosophy that the best way for us to learn was from our mistakes. We got bumped and bruised and we all have the odd scar to show. However, life on the farm, with Thistle Island as our backyard playground, helped us become more resilient, fearless and tough – useful attributes for handling life experiences.

Brother Mark remembers his mum and dad were generally alert to potential dangers:

> Our parents encouraged us to explore, but always showed us the risks. I remember when we as kids went to Fossil Point on Thistle Island, where the waves come crashing in from the Southern Ocean. Dad didn't just tell us to be careful. He took us to the edge of the cliffs, not to scare us, but to point down to the rocks far below. The message was clear. We all remember Dad saying, many times, 'Never turn your back on the sea.' There was one time though when I think even Dad was scared. We were flying in our Cessna over water. About halfway to the island the engine started to cough and die. It seemed that we had run out of fuel. At age ten (Kieran was eight) I knew this was not good. While Dad was going through the pilot's checklist and examining the gauges I noticed that Kieran was busy with something between the seats. He had found the fuel tap and was happily playing with it, turning it on and off and on and off.

Active children use lots of energy; mealtimes were important for nourishment *and* rest. For breakfast we chose Weet-Bix. Due to large appetites there had to be breakfast rules. Each child could have as many Weet-Bix as could fit in a dessert bowl, but were not allowed a refill. A sub-rule was that a half-teaspoon of sugar was allowed for each two biscuits. Weet-Bix can soak up a lot of milk and we managed to add so much of this that our parents started using milk powder instead. Breakfast time saw us quietly and meticulously stacking Weet-Bix into a bowl, carefully adding milk to each layer, with just a sprinkle of sugar. We certainly were 'Weet-Bix kids'.

School was not much fun for me. I caught the bus to Port Lincoln and, probably like many kids, couldn't wait to be on the bus home. Because my birthdate just missed the cut-off for entry into reception, I was nearly a year older than most of my classmates, so school should have been easier for me. I began to fall behind the others academically and because I lost interest, I played up. I was labelled 'naughty' and 'mischievous' and put into a special class. I was struggling to read the blackboard but I assumed the other kids were having the same problem. Before my deteriorating sight was diagnosed, I was easily distracted and in one class was sent to sit at the back of the room so I was less of a distraction to others. What I could see on the blackboard from this position is anybody's guess!

This continued until Port Lincoln Junior Primary School received a visit from Jan Waller, a nurse responsible for regular juvenile health check-ups. She formed the opinion that my learning and behaviour problems stemmed from the fact I couldn't see properly, and suggested a referral to a visiting Whyalla ophthalmologist. I didn't cooperate during the tests, so the ophthalmologist decided I was a naughty boy, but my eyes were fine!

My parents and Nurse Waller weren't satisfied with this diagnosis. There followed visits to other eye specialists until Dr Harold Handley, an Adelaide ophthalmologist, diagnosed a vision impairment called juvenile optic atrophy.

Optic atrophy is the term used to describe the loss of a proportion of optic disc nerve fibres. It is characterised by optic disc pallor, loss of acuity, loss of colour vision, as well as defects in the field of vision called centrocecal (central) scotomas. We all have a very small scotoma or a 'blind spot', but in Kieran's case this is large and central in both eyes. Interestingly, juvenile optic atrophy is more prevalent in girls and often does not manifest itself until the second decade of life. Kieran's mum and dad had no idea about his condition until Jan Waller visited his school when he was eight years old.

On reflection, Mum noted I played games of every nature with my siblings without apparent difficulty. I even managed marbles, but in hindsight, this was perhaps because they were moving objects and I could use my peripheral vision to look down on the action. Similarly, I can play table tennis, but struggle with tennis. Squash is good because the black ball moves around four white walls and when I played night tennis, I could see the bright ball ... unless it was coming straight at me!

Dad was intrigued that I liked to look very, very closely at small objects like wristwatches. But he also liked to do this, so this behaviour hadn't seemed extraordinary either. It's difficult to determine when my sight began failing. If you lose a limb it is immediately evident. But no one notices when you gradually lose your sight. I probably had quite good vision to start with and the blindness came on as I grew older. Perhaps the only early indication that my vision was failing occurred in our kitchen at home while watching TV. I liked to get close to it, and Mum would say, 'Kieran, move your chair back.' I would do as I was told, but gradually the chair would creep closer and closer to the TV. My eyes had been tested by an optometrist in Port Lincoln and I had spectacles already. I guess everyone assumed that even though my vision was clearly not perfect, it wasn't going to be a major problem. In those days, the equipment used was nowhere near as sophisticated as it is today, and my condition is extremely rare. The glasses may have helped by cleaning up the lens distortion but would have done nothing for my developing vision impairment.

The damage to the optic nerve would explain the difficulties I was having learning to read and write at school. My brain was not always receiving the full signal, so I was only seeing parts of the letters and numbers.

One of my survival strategies was to be a follower. When at home I followed Darren and Mark around. Everything I did was an attempt to keep up with them. I did the same at school, copying what others were doing.

Once I had been diagnosed, my family and the medical specialists wanted to know the origin of the eye problem. I was probably told why I was being tested, but was too young to fully understand. There was a fair bit of fuss made over me and I didn't know why. Soon I found myself being driven back to Adelaide for further tests. I remember having drops put in my eyes and visiting lots of medical clinics. I was intrigued by the strange equipment, but it wasn't stressful and I was enjoying the extra attention. Mum is tall and takes long, quick strides, and I found myself half-walking, half-running to keep up with her as we went from one waiting room to another. But it was a big Adelaide adventure and a whole lot better than being at school. The conclusion was I had simply been born with the condition. Now that everyone knew my issue, the support began.

Townsend House is an excellent facility in Adelaide for people like me. After a visit to the experts there, I returned to Port Lincoln Primary School, to complete Year 5, with aids to help me see and read more effectively.

June Burt (from Townsend House school) visited me once a year to check on my progress and communicate with my teachers. June wanted to do this on a term-by-term basis, but the principal queried the action saying I was one of the leaders in sport, and when I played footy, I had no problem seeing the ball. June asked him to change the footy to a tennis ball and then to observe my dexterity, but the school insisted. June backed off, and I continued to receive her annual visit. Fortunately I was doing much better at school anyway.

(Author) Uncle Andy: *Your Auntie Marlene and I were living in Port Lincoln at the time and were both teachers at your primary school. You were taught by friends of ours, motivated, capable and professional people. I'm surprised your optic atrophy wasn't picked up sooner.*

Kieran: Well, no one in my family spotted it either. I didn't know what was happening and was very keen to hide my problems and fit in with my peer group.

When your mum and dad had to go away for a week, they asked us to babysit you all. Do you remember that?

Yes ... vaguely. Were we good?

Well to be honest, you were all very energetic and a bit difficult to handle. There didn't seem to be too many ground rules, except for the Weet-Bix ones. I love playing games and I remember playing build-up chasey with you all.

We loved it when our rellies joined in games. Could you catch me?

I could at that time. I wouldn't want to try now. You were quite small then, but still very fast. Actually I made a point of catching you first, because although you were slower than your brothers, you were determined – and just a little bit stubborn.

What do you mean stubborn, and how did that help you?

Well, once caught in build-up chasey, you have to help catch the others – and that's where you excelled. Once you got on the trail of either of your brothers, you just did not give up and eventually ran them down. That kind of determination is a pretty useful trait to have.

I loved it at home, and on the island, but that's about to change, isn't it?

2 Adelaide and the car ride

1983–1987

In 1983, when I was 11 years old, it was decided I needed to attend the school at Townsend House in Adelaide full-time and so board there. This would have meant I was away from home for three months at a time, but fortunately the South Australian Government stepped in and flew me back to Port Lincoln on alternate weekends. Apparently, my brothers and sister were jealous of these flights, but not surprisingly I was finding it difficult to adjust to living in Adelaide.

It was late evening when I arrived at my boarding cottage at Townsend for the first time. Here I was introduced to my cottage mother, Mrs Scott, in the foyer. Compared to home, there was a lot of noise and activity. Our housemother was nice, but it wasn't really a parental role – in the circumstances it probably couldn't be. As a boarding facility (there were seven cottages altogether; five for the deaf and two for the blind), the cottage had strict rules. In the morning before I could go to breakfast I had to dress, make my bed and vacuum my room. It was always a race to see who could get the vacuum cleaner first. Once our rooms were checked, we could go to breakfast. After school and on weekends we did our own washing and ironing, and there were dishes to wash and dry after every meal. We helped ourselves to breakfasts, so I could indulge my Weet-Bix habit, and the cook made sure the biscuit and cake tins were always full. But it was so controlled and I was used to freedom at home. I was very lonely, especially at night-time. Lights out was strictly 9.30 pm, the beds were hard, and I would lie for hours wondering what was happening to me and wishing I was back at home.

As a person who likes a little mischief and pranking, I would sometimes hide from the staff. I felt I was safely out of sight behind a plant box or a low wall, but I was always getting caught. It took a long time for me to work out their sight was much better than mine. They must have thought it quite funny to see this skinny little kid trying to hide behind an even skinnier tree. But I did get better at it. When I got upset I would go for a walk. In the city, I couldn't go far without crossing busy roads and I wasn't confident enough to do this, so I would walk around the block. This was not far enough. On one occasion, after doing only one lap of the block, I could hear a search party out looking for me. I wasn't ready to go back so I sat in the middle of some pampas grass, this time well hidden. I had a lot of issues to deal with, I often felt rebellious, and I really missed the care of my family.

School in Adelaide was quite different as well. It was a shock. From a class of 25 students at Port Lincoln Primary School, I was now in a class of only nine with Miss Harris. I felt I had been doing fine in Port Lincoln, and didn't think there were any problems.

Kieran's cottage mother Peggy Scott clearly remembers how unhappy he was:

> Kieran found it hard to adjust and the first three months were hell for him. He got into a bit of trouble, but I wouldn't say he was naughty. He was just angry and couldn't understand why he'd been sent away to live with 'retards'. He thought he was normal and most of the other children in the house had

> more obvious disabilities. Some could get quite violent. I think when he returned home at the end of the first term he was reminded how his parents loved him, and when he returned to us he began to settle down. Kieran had a lovely teacher at Townsend who tutored him and helped him catch up with his school studies. She encouraged and praised him and he began to progress.

His parents were also adjusting to his long absences from home:

> It was a huge shock for us. We knew Kieran was unhappy at his new school and we missed him at home. It was a feeling of despair and we tried everything we could to make Kieran feel better about himself and his new learning environment. We noticed a big lift in his spirits when he threw himself into athletics, and we would travel across to Adelaide to support him whenever we could.

I attended Townsend at an opportune time for anyone like me who was interested in sport. Peggy Scott and others there were getting us out into local special interest clubs.

Dennis Peck and Jenny Flood were the organisers of the sports and physical education section at Townsend school and both were great motivators. Dennis was a gymnastics instructor at Seacliff Youth Centre and enjoyed working with his new charges from Townsend. Inspired by visually impaired kids, he had changed occupations to work at Townsend as the PE specialist and then mobility teacher:

> I first met Kieran when he came with his dad and brothers to Townsend to see if Kieran could fit in at the school and the cottage. The three boys looked very fit and athletic, so I got them to run around the oval and see if my assessment was accurate. They were all very good, but I knew straight away Kieran was a natural.

Jenny Flood was a junior primary classroom teacher at Townsend school and rekindled her love of running when the school needed extra guide runners for the City to Bay (Adelaide to Glenelg) Fun Run. Guide runners run alongside the visually impaired (VI) athletes, each runner holding the end of a short rope. Much practice is required for this to work effectively. After school finished, Jenny and Dennis ran gymnastic classes at the school and athletic training sessions on Saturday mornings. Jenny remembers:

> Kieran was a natural athlete in a wonderful athletic environment. Dennis worked as a specialist in physical education, and sport was a curriculum priority. Between Kieran's cottage and the school was an oval especially set up for VI sport and training. We had loads of the latest in sports equipment, and there was a lot of extra-curricular sport – in fact, everything was on tap. Kieran took full advantage of these excellent facilities and blossomed with encouragement.

The school placed great emphasis on music and sport because these activities were not so sight-reliant. Although deteriorating quickly, my sight wasn't bad enough at this stage for me to enter competitions solely for VI athletes. Dennis and Jenny introduced me to the City to Bay Fun Run and it was the ideal challenge. At the age of 11 and basically untrained, I surprised Dennis by running the 12 km in under an hour. For seven years in a row I trained for and entered the annual City to Bay, with a best time of 46 minutes. I became hooked on athletics; I learned what was needed to compete, improve and succeed, and it helped to build my self-confidence.

Dennis and Jenny were instrumental in organising a South Australian team for vision-impaired championships at state and national levels. They accompanied these squads and had a lot to do with Kieran's success. Dennis credits the role of the parents:

> South Australia used to send only bowlers and cricketers to the Blind Nationals and I was asked to organise an athletics squad. Our first team had only six members – but they entered nearly every event. They were understandably exhausted at the end of the meet, but we showed the other states what we could do. We went on to be the top state for many years with up to 40 squad members. I believe our success was due mainly to our parents. They really got behind their VI children and gave them extra training on top of our sessions.

Matters didn't always go as planned. At a discus training session at Townsend, I nearly decapitated Dennis. Many VI athletes stand and after a few arm swings, spin out the discus. However, I soon discovered I could throw much further when I did a body spin before releasing the discus. On this particular day I got slightly disorientated in the swing and the discus emerged – off course by 90 degrees. Dennis, standing close by and directly in the path of the missile, did not even have time to duck. A very white-faced and shaken coach retreated to safety before my next throw.

Jenny was a great admirer of Kieran, but so were others:

> Kieran was a wonderful role model for the younger students especially. He showed everyone, including the parents of blind children, what could be done with determination and a fair dose of ability. With his lovely nature and manners, his friendliness and good looks – not to forget all his muscles – he was very popular with the girls.

Ann Baillie, Dennis's wife, taught at Townsend for 31 years. Many years after Kieran left, she invited him back to talk to her upper primary class, and during his presentation realised some of the children had no idea what his muscles looked like. Ann asked Millie, a totally blind student, if she would like to feel them. Kieran played along and the class loved it when Millie felt Kieran's (very well developed) calf muscles and called out, 'What are they?'

At age 14 my sight had deteriorated to a point that made me eligible to attend the 1986 Blind National Games in Sydney. I started to do well at athletics. Everywhere I went on the sporting field, I knew my vision impairment was a disadvantage, so to beat athletes with normal vision was an accomplishment. I wasn't too fazed about winning, I just wanted to beat as many contestants as I could. It was a big driving force, and suddenly my disadvantage didn't matter. I developed a fascination with the javelin. Keeping a few in the cottage and being so close to the school, I could practice throwing the javelin after school on the oval.

From 1983 to 1985 Kieran won the champion trophies for the Townsend school sports days and swimming carnivals. However, this growing self-confidence was about to take a hit.

After my primary school education at Townsend, I moved to neighbouring Mawson High School for secondary schooling. Here my handicap felt more pronounced. My deteriorating sight meant I found it difficult to see facial expressions and body language, and I struggled to read people. I felt at a great disadvantage. At Townsend I had some control over the situation, because I could see people better than most. I had eventually settled down, and got along well with the students and staff. At Mawson, I was surrounded by hundreds of kids who could see me better than I could see them. Peer group pressure was huge. I tried to disguise my condition, while at the same time closely observing these new people who acted quite differently from those with whom I had lived before.

Suddenly I felt fearful, vulnerable, self-conscious and embarrassed. I became very careful and calculated with my movements. It was a tricky and exhausting time learning to socialise and fit in. But I was really only bluffing myself and I had to later unlearn a lot of this stuff and accept who I was so that I could move forward.

I do remember one incident at this school which changed a few attitudes – most importantly my own. There was a largish boy who liked to tease me, call me names and run off. I took it for a while, but on this one day I chased and somehow tripped him. He fell badly, got to his feet with a bloodied nose, and came at me with fists swinging. I had done some judo, so I picked him up, put him over my shoulder, lay him down on his back and said, 'That's enough.' I noticed from that moment on I got more respect from him and the group. It was to be my only fight and I would never condone this behaviour. But I had used an asset I previously overlooked – my strength. I became increasingly active in sport, where I didn't have to hide my impairment so carefully. My attitude became more positive. It was like stepping out of the shadows.

With this new attitude I went to an athletics tryout day sponsored by the sugar industry. The coaches running the event didn't know I was visually impaired, so I tried the pole vault and enjoyed it. People thought it was dangerous, but I wasn't scared at all. I had been brought up to try new things and handle knocks. I was disappointed that when we went rock climbing in Adelaide, they attached me to a safety harness and safety lines. I was used to climbing the cliffs at Thistle Island without them. It was part of the challenge and added to the adrenalin rush.

At Mawson High, my athletic ability was noticed by a man who was to play a vital role in my athletic career.

John Hamann was a technical studies teacher at the school. As well as looking after his Year Ten care group, he was scouting athletes for selection in the Interschool Team, which would compete against 16 other schools in the upcoming Secondary School Sport South Australia (SSSSA) Carnival. John well remembers the day he spotted Kieran's talent:

> Every year during the first week of March, Mawson High School held its Athletics Day on the school oval. We arranged the competition in year level groups, with the students competing in track and field in the morning, and a variety of ball games after lunch. I first noticed Kieran during a Year 8 400-metre event. He won the event easily, so I approached him to ask for his name and class in order to include him in our squad. Kieran was built much more strongly than the other students his age, and had the most pleasant of smiles and manners. He told me he would like to be in the school squad. Kieran went on to win several more events during the day and our relationship began.
>
> During the next three years I taught him woodwork, metalwork and plastics technology. Because of his interest in the outdoors and his wonderful natural ability to do things well, I also became his athletics coach. I would drive him to the Olympic Sports Field, twice a week to begin with, so he could train for his running events. He would later train four times a week and compete on some Saturday afternoons during our summer interclub.

I continued to live in the Townsend Cottage, but I was now the only secondary student there and living with children attending primary school.

The Modra family have a long and valued relationship with Immanuel College in Novar Gardens, a suburb south-west of Adelaide and very near the delightful seaside city of Glenelg. As a Lutheran secondary school with boarding facilities, it was well patronised by families living in country South Australia, and all of Theo's brothers and sisters had studied there. Kieran's parents felt it was time for him to have this experience as well. They also saw the importance of Kieran living with people his own age. And so, after six years, Kieran's Townsend experience concluded, although he was to continue to use their services.

Peggy and her dog, Katie, were sad to see him go:

> I didn't want to part with him. I know you are not supposed to have favourites, but some kids can be loved a little bit more and Kieran was with me a long time. He did come back a few times for weekends and that was wonderful. Katie, my dog, missed Kieran as well. Of all the children I had in the house, Kieran was the only one whose lap Katie chose to sit on. She would go out with him when he was training. He would throw the javelin, then the discus, and then Katie's frisbee. When she died, we buried her in the cottage garden where she had spent many hours with her favourite, Kieran.

Eventually the Townsend school and cottages became too expensive for the state education department to maintain. It was decided to establish a more central Adelaide school for these children. Ascot Park Primary School had plenty of area, but was struggling with enrolments, so the South Australian School for Vision Impaired (SASVI) was relocated to share their grounds. The service arm of the organisation stayed at Townsend House and was given a new name – Can:Do 4Kids. This remains a family-centred service providing quality specialist programs for children and young people across South Australia. Much of the land where Kieran spent years of his childhood living and training is now a retirement village.

Peggy retired in 1998 after 33 years as a cottage mother. Peggy, who has reverted to her maiden name of Bell, was advised by doctors to stop riding her bike at age 75. Her dedication to those in her care was legendary. She got 'her children' involved in all sorts of clubs and hobbies. She took them on camps and to pretty much every educational and tourist attraction around Adelaide. She always drove Kieran to the airport for his trips home, and picked him up on his return. Peggy was a wonderful 'mum', and like all mums, her love for Kieran and her charges was boundless.

Peggy took them to music lessons and even got them to sing together:

> The cottages had their own choir and would sometimes put on concerts at the school to raise money for equipment. They also joined the choir at St Jude's Anglican Church nearby in Brighton. Their choir conductor, a lovely person named Sister Jean, would come back to the cottages to help teach the children. Those children could really sing.

I have mixed feelings about Townsend. I remember how desperately isolated I once felt. On the farm I had space and access to many vehicles, and had become a competent driver. On one evening at Townsend I was feeling frustrated, angry, confined and rebellious. I snuck out and took the Sister's car for a 5 km drive down the road and back again! Nobody ever found out. If they had, I hate to think how much trouble I would have been in. It was night-time with next to no traffic and I only drove around the back streets, but I was 12 years old and it was a crazy thing to do, and probably sums up my state of mind at that time.

However I also appreciate the help and love that I received there. Looking back, I think this institution was the best place for me because I didn't feel out of place. After the initial problems I didn't have to worry about peer group pressure because everyone was going through a similar situation. It was a time when I was learning a lot about who I was. My cottage mum was wonderful, the people there were friendly, and the excellent teachers helped me catch up on my academic skills and introduced me to so many different experiences and sports.

At Immanuel College, I finished Year 10 and proceeded to Year 11. I was then given permission to do Year 12 over two years – the first student there to be given this advantage.

Living in the close confines of the boarding house, where six boys often shared a room, was a challenge for me. When the kids came back to the dormitories after school, they were relaxed and could 'let their hair down'. But I was always trying to suppress my impairment. I felt they were staring at me, particularly when I used my monocular or pulled my books close to my face to read them. I didn't have a lot of self-confidence and quietly stayed in the background. I was never bullied, but felt I couldn't fully relax or relate easily to other students. This might have been an overreaction from me because I was so sensitive at the time.

I moved out of the boarding house after my first year of Year 12, and found rental accommodation a kilometre from the school. Students and staff selected school prefects, and I was thrilled to become one in Year 13. While at Immanuel, John Hamann continued to coach me.

John encouraged and helped Kieran to improve and progress:

> Kieran just loved training. As he prospered, he tried other events and we found he could throw a javelin well, so we

allocated more time to this. Soon he was throwing as well as the other athletes he was training with.

In 1987 I was chosen for the Pan Pacific Games in New Zealand as a para-athlete for the javelin event. The selectors of the newly developed Australian Paralympic team were now noticing me.

The term Paralympic first came into use for the Seoul Olympics in 1988. This term is derived from the Greek preposition 'para' meaning 'beside' or 'alongside', referring to a competition held in parallel with the Olympic Games. After Seoul, any city bidding for the Olympic Games was obliged to include the Paralympic Games in their submission, and so these new games benefited from the same organisational structure as the Olympic Games.

Athletes with disabilities did compete in the Olympic Games prior to the advent of the Paralympics. In 1948 in London, Dr Ludwig Guttmann (who had been helped to flee Nazi Germany in 1939) organised a sports competition called the Stoke Mandeville Games, which involved British World War II veterans who had spinal injuries. These Games were held in the same location in 1952, and Dutch veterans were invited, making it the first international competition of its kind. These early competitions have been described as the precursors of the Paralympic Games, and the 2012 London Paralympics celebrated its sixtieth anniversary. In 1960 well-organised Paralympics were conducted using Olympic venues in Rome and then four years later the games were held in Tokyo. For the next 20 years until Seoul, the Paralympics venues were not aligned with the Olympic movement, being held in Israel, West Germany, Canada, the Netherlands, the United Kingdom and the United States. From the Seoul Games onwards, the Summer Paralympic Games were conducted generally about two to three weeks after the Summer Olympics finished and at the same venue.

At the tender age of 16, I was selected to represent Australia at the 1988 Seoul Paralympics – the youngest member in the team. There weren't the same criteria to qualify back then. I wasn't chasing qualifying times like I need to today. I was trying to balance schoolwork with athletics, and I needed encouragement from Mum and Dad to go. They told me it was a once-in-a-lifetime experience.

Uncle Andy: *Leaving home must have been heart-breaking, but it probably forced you to face up to and handle your disability sooner – and Adelaide certainly offered you opportunities to try out different sports and experiences.*

Kieran: With hindsight you're right, but I would have given that up to spend more time with my family on the farm. I was lucky to be cared for by some terrific people in Adelaide but I didn't always behave well.

I've met up with many of the people mentioned so far in the book. They all have great respect and love for you.

Yes, I realise that now, and if I could go back to those days with a little more maturity and understanding, I might do things differently. But coming to terms with a disability, such as my growing blindness, was and is a constant challenge. My eyes are still changing and I'm still adapting.

Do you feel guilty about taking the car for a joyride? I did consider leaving that out of the book because it is a serious offence.

It has to be in the book. It happened and we both want this to be an honest, open and transparent account of my life. I don't think I felt guilt. I was used to driving vehicles around the farm and felt capable and safe. But it was impulsive, foolhardy and dangerous. We all make mistakes and need to learn from them, and this wasn't to be the last mistake I made.

The children in your family have all been given a chance to go to boarding school. It seems to me that most of you didn't enjoy it much.

I'm not sure why we didn't adapt as well as others. Maybe we were so used to the freedom of the farm we couldn't handle all the rules and regulations. Tania and Darren adapted a little better – they were more academic. Our biggest disadvantage was that we were only sent to boarding school for the last two years, and by then most of the boarders had established friendships. You'd think I would have handled it better after living away from home from the age of 11. Since then I've stayed in many dormitories and camps and managed okay – well, not always, as our readers are about to find out ...

3 Seoul and pole vaulting

1988–1991

I am not one to make excuses, but in Seoul I didn't feel competitive. Still coming to terms with my own disability, I lacked the confidence and the edge that is needed to succeed. It was my first Paralympics campaign and I was more shell-shocked than anything. At school I was trying to hide my disability, but my disability was why I was at the Games. It was out in the open and I had to deal with it.

Surrounded by people speaking strange languages, and with all the cultural experiences that South Korea offered, my sport took a back seat. I was mesmerised by the Korean culture. Not sure what to do, I followed another Australian javelin-thrower, John Domandl. I was shocked when I saw some of the slum areas, and I didn't know how to handle my freedom. At the age of 16, I could buy a bottle of rum at a street stall. At the Pan Pacific Games, everything was tightly organised and controlled. In Seoul, I was largely left to make my own decisions, and I found myself focusing more on the culture around me than my sport. There weren't a lot of spectators and those there were mainly schoolkids. They would rush up and ask for autographs, which helped my self-confidence.

It was an era when the focus of the Paralympic movement was to encourage disabled athletes and allow them the opportunity to share the experiences of able-bodied sportspeople. The emphasis was on the process rather than on the outcome. Any medals were a bonus.

A good example of this philosophy was to be a lasting memory and future motivation for me. I was encouraged to compete in any events, so I chose the 1500 m, without having the necessary specialised training and preparation. I had no idea how fast these athletes ran and ended way back in the field, finishing dead last. I was embarrassed and resolved to be better prepared in future.

My own event, the javelin, was held on a field outside the main stadium that lacked atmosphere. I didn't have a coach present and without experience I came sixth, but was happy with the result.

Back in Adelaide, coach John Hamann was following Kieran's progress and knew he could do better, but was also aware of how big the Seoul stage was:

> I was hoping he would medal with a javelin throw of around 55 m in Seoul, but he threw just over 50 m to finish sixth in the Open event. It was still an incredible performance for his first big competition.

It was also one of my earliest experiences of being with hundreds of people with more obvious disabilities. I found myself staring. I still do, but now I really appreciate them, and am interested in their story and their journey. It's kind of strange, but when I'm away from the Games I try to look normal. When I'm competing at the Games I try to look disabled, because there is always the fear someone might protest if you appear to have more functional ability than expected. A normal athlete competing as disabled is one of the biggest forms of cheating in the Games.

This extreme form of cheating was to be exposed later at the 2000 Summer Paralympics in Sydney. Spain was stripped of their intellectual disability basketball gold medals shortly after the Games closed, when

Carlos Ribagorda – a member of the victorious team and an undercover journalist – revealed to the Spanish business magazine Capital *that most of his colleagues had not undergone cognitive tests to ensure they had a disability. Ten of the 12 competitors in the team were not disabled.*

There was scant reporting of the Seoul Paralympics back in Australia and when I returned to school, little was made of my trip, which I was quite happy about. I was asked to talk briefly to the students at my school and being one of my first experiences in public speaking, I memorised my whole speech. As often happens, I forgot half of what I intended to say when I got up on stage for the presentation. There was also a parade down Adelaide's main thoroughfare, King William Street, with cars and balloons and a healthy crowd, which did make me feel honoured.

Back in training with John Hamann at Kensington Park, I was trying another sport – pole vaulting – purely for the adrenalin rush. Mr Hamann was always encouraging and took me from vaulting with a long broomstick in a sandpit through to the real thing. He made sure I mastered each skill thoroughly before progressing. But he didn't limit me. I was surprised and impressed by this. Mr Hamann would pick me up at Immanuel on his way to Kensington Park. I don't think many people there knew I had problems with my vision. I would put a shoe at the start of my run-up. A pole vaulter running at full pace generally lowers the pole from the horizontal about 3 paces from the vault box where the pole is planted. I couldn't see a vault box from three paces away so I needed another shoe next to the vault box.

John knew he needed to be careful as he introduced Kieran to this potentially dangerous sport:

> Not long after Seoul, Kieran's javelin throwing had to be reduced because he injured his elbow, and so his pole-vaulting training increased. When he first started vaulting, I took him through all the usual drills and short run-up jumps that all vaulters do. However, to make sure he didn't hurt himself, I made him do them over and over again for many months more than the other vaulters. I wanted to be sure that his run-up, plant of the pole, and take off were all automatic and well defined in his brain. He took about three times longer than usual to learn the sport, but he doesn't dwell on fear. He used our Nordic training poles more than any other athlete will ever use them. With some reluctance, I introduced him to our UCS Spirit competition poles so he could start to feel the benefit of the lighter, but stronger, rebounding competition poles. Well, he took to them like a duck to water. It seemed they were made for each other as he kept on jumping higher and higher. Other vaulters from all around Australia could not believe he was visually impaired. He was a true champion – proud, thrilled, but humble.

Even though the pole-vaulting group with whom I trained and competed were a nice group of people, I felt inferior to them. I knew I was missing some things with my impairment. After two years of training and competition, I won the Australian National Under 19 title in pole-vaulting at the 1989 Australian All Schools Track and Field Championships against able-bodied athletes. This remains one of my most memorable sporting highlights and was an enormous boost to my confidence. I vaulted 4.45 m – 20 cm more than my previous best – and just missed a 4.60 m. There was a good crowd supporting me and I enjoyed the moment. I stood very tall that day.

John Hamann rates this win as Kieran's finest:

> I believe this was Kieran's greatest sporting achievement. He was up against some really good kids, who went on to represent Australia at Commonwealth Games in the pole vault.

Selected in the South Australian Under 18 team for pole vault, I travelled to athletic events around Australia. In Queensland, I had a frightening experience. At the athletics track there was one grandstand only. The venue was in a flat area and the sports field was surrounded by clear, blue sky, rather than the gum trees I was used to. For the first time I could see the bar, and how high it was! I got very scared and began to doubt myself. It took me some time to get rid of the fear and vault with any confidence. Back at my home training track the bar was camouflaged by large gum trees, so somehow it didn't seem so high off the ground. My coach must have wondered what was going on and probably thought I was overawed by competing interstate.

To help me the officials had painted the 'mouse' (the vault box) white, but as you would expect, an athlete pole vaulting with 15% vision is almost bound to have accidents, and I certainly did. I couldn't see the bar from the end of my run-up, so I would stand under it, look up at it and then count out my steps. Once running in, I would look for the vault box and then the bar on my way up. At training, I remember that I missed the mouse to the left. I managed to get airborne, only to find the pole was pushing me further left. As I was coming down I just managed to clip the side of the mat and then it was straight on to concrete. I had a badly bruised hip for a long time. I had a more embarrassing fall at a competition and in front of my fellow competitors and spectators. I tore down the runway and missed the mouse again. This time the end of the pole got stuck between the mats. It felt okay so I started upward and had my feet pointing well, but the pole was unstable and couldn't support my weight. I fell flat on my back on the track and felt very foolish!

A partially sighted person excelling at pole vaulting is newsworthy and attracted the attention of media personality Derryn Hinch, who interviewed Kieran at Kensington Park for Hinch, *his Channel 7 television program.*

Fortunately, Kieran's all-round athletics ability had made him well-known at State and National level. Not only skilled in javelin throwing and pole vaulting, he was now proficient in long jump and triple jump. He was proud to be awarded the 1989 Eyre Peninsula Sportsperson of the Year Award presented in Port Lincoln on Australia Day, an award that bears such famous names as Dean Lukin, John Fitzgerald and no doubt Kyle Chalmers soon. This award presented by the Port Lincoln Rotary Club was also to be given to his sister Tania many years later.

Sean Carlin, who represented Australia at the Barcelona and Atlanta Olympics and had won two gold medals at the Commonwealth Games in 1990 and 1994, coached Kieran in hammer throwing.

Sean was an amazing hammer thrower and a great guy. We got along very well and I was doing okay – when I let the hammer go at the right time. After one season, I qualified for the Under 18 Nationals and then made the state team as a hammer thrower. I found that with poor vision I got easily disorientated while I was spinning. On one occasion, I let the hammer go too early and it went clean through the side of a nearby shed.

At the 1991 Blind Sports Federation national titles over Easter, Kieran came first in five events – the triple jump with an Australian record of 11.9 m, the 200 m and 1500 m, discus and javelin, and in the pool he came second in the 50 m freestyle. He continued to enjoy Immanuel College sports days. A record of 13.61 m that Kieran set in the 1991 senior boy's shot put (5 kg) stood for 21 years and was broken by Thomas Marshall in 2012 at the Knockout Cup competition when he pushed 14.13 m.

I was offered a scholarship at the Canberra AIS, but turned it down to complete my Year 12 studies at Immanuel. I still felt I could do better in javelin. In Australia, Russell Short and John Domandl were throwing further, but I was much younger than both and still growing.

My athletic career was about to hit a hurdle, or perhaps I should say a badminton net. At school we would do crazy stuff. We saw this badminton net and the middle of it was sagging a bit, so I decided to jump over it. I made it over but landed bent-legged. I tore some cartilage in my left knee and this still causes me problems, but mainly when I don't exercise. The knee seems to be better when the muscles around it are strong. I tried to ignore the pain from my elbow and knee, but clearly javelin throwing was not helping those injuries heal. So, I took time out to have arthroscopic surgery to clean up torn cartilage. As I have done on many occasions, I sought advice from John Hamann.

John remembers how desperately keen Kieran was to continue with his sport:

> After his operation he came out to the Olympic Sports Field to talk to me about what he should do for rehabilitation, as he desperately wanted to continue his Paralympic dreams. I told him that he would not be able to throw the javelin for nine or ten months, as the knees supply quite a lot of the braking and power for the javelin just before the arm throws it. Pole vaulting

> would have to wait for months as well, and anyway it was not a Paralympic event for AWDs (Athletes with Disabilities). I suggested he keep on walking as much as possible and to take up swimming, an excellent exercise for bringing knees back to strength. I think it was about this time that Tania, his younger sister, began at Immanuel as well. She too was quite a good athlete and simply followed along like Kieran and did well in most events. Anyway, Kieran joined the morning and afternoon swimmers and swam to his heart's content. Just like in athletics, he thrived in the water and was soon swimming fast times in a variety of styles.

I swam purely to keep fit, but the coaches there kept encouraging me to swim faster and I enjoy challenges. They said I was okay, so I swam in the South Australian State Swimming Championships in Adelaide. I had applied unsuccessfully for university, so when Ian McDowell-Jones, a swimming coach from Sydney, offered to coach me, I accepted.

Kieran had taken the opportunity to prepare himself for his future by working conscientiously at Immanuel College. Other than sport, his interests were music, art, photography, craft and pottery. Kieran's Year 12 results were very good. Over his time there he had gained a certificate in 'Young Achievement Business Experience' with Onya Industries in 1989. In 1990 he came first in Photography and gained an Outstanding Achievement award in Art, and in 1991 he was equal first in the Echo (college magazine) photography competition.

Coach John Hamann was most impressed with this latter award:

> I taught Kieran photography at Mawson High in the days when we shot and developed black and white photos. Kieran thought he was pretty good at it, but he couldn't see and most of his images were out of focus and a bit askew. To develop black

> and white photos you had to work in a dark room, look hard and concentrate. Of course, this didn't suit a young boy who was losing his eyesight and I don't believe I ever saw him take a good photo. The news that he had won awards at Immanuel for photography was just incredible!

I needed a break from all the study and now had a disability pension and therefore the means to survive financially. So off to Sydney I went and I loved the hustle and bustle of Australia's largest city. I rode my bike and was always mindful of the drainage grates in Sydney roads, which run parallel to the streets and are a nasty trap for bike tyres. As well as being coached in swimming, I helped Ian (McDowell-Jones) by being a swimming instructor at the Lindfield Swimming School and went back to study to gain a certificate in Exercise Physiology Management at the University of New South Wales.

After my time in Sydney, I was offered more swimming coaching at the Australian Institute of Sport in Canberra under Anne Green. She introduced me to the Telopea Swim Club and provided my accommodation, but I wasn't always the model student. I was quite a handful. I struggled with the intensity of training twice every day. I couldn't see my improvement. Much younger swimmers would pass me so easily. I didn't have their finesse, just sheer strength. I would have to get up at 4.30 am to ride 12 km to the Institute and it was fiercely cold. After two hours of swimming I would ride the 12 km home. In the afternoon I would do that all again. I missed training sessions, was given warnings, had difficulty getting to the qualifying times and nearly missed out on going to Barcelona. I much preferred riding my bike around Canberra and checking out the many tourist attractions.

Uncle Andy: *You must be very proud of your pole-vaulting achievements, especially in open competition.*

Kieran: That was a wonderful boost for me and a real adrenalin rush. But at that stage of my life my body shape was changing. The more I trained, the more muscle I put on and sometimes this made it difficult.

With all those muscles and medallions, you must have been attracting some attention from girls. Did you have a special girlfriend?

I enjoyed the company of girls and related well to them as friends. But I was very focused on my sport and I think I was just too shy to single one out.

Is there any sport that you tried, but didn't do well in?

Not really, but of course I was limited by my eyesight. At that time in my life I was kind of swimming with the tide. When a door opened, I walked through it, but I was becoming frustrated because I knew I needed a career – and in my sport, I was not improving as quickly as I would have liked.

Hang in there, Kieran. You are about to find the sport – and the girl.

It's just as well she wasn't as shy as me! Well, she probably was ... but her friends weren't!

4 Barcelona and the girl

1992–1995

All the swimming training in Sydney and Canberra must have worked because at the 12th Australian Championships for the Blind, held in Adelaide in January 1992, Kieran excelled. He collected six gold medals in backstroke, freestyle and the medley and broke the Australian record in four of these events. He added two bronze medals, swimming for South Australia in the relays. Just to prove that he could still do it, he won another gold in the javelin and a silver in the hammer throw.

Andrew Denton, host of Live and Sweaty, a sports program on ABC TV, had heard of a South Australian athlete with only 15% vision who had competed successfully in all manner of sports – including pole vaulting! In August 1992 Kieran appeared on national television.

I got into the spirit of the show. The whole idea is that you are serious – and he is funny (well he is anyway!) – and he takes the mickey out of you. It was kind of uncomfortable, but good fun as well.

While at the Institute of Sport, I had continued my javelin throwing under the tutelage of former Commonwealth Games athlete, Chris Nunn. However, I was primarily selected in the Barcelona Paralympic team as a 50 m freestyle swimmer.

Impressed as I was with the way the Spanish had set up the Olympic–Paralympic venue, I was really disappointed in my own attitude at the start of my event. I stood on the blocks for the 50 m and I didn't feel edgy or excited. There was no adrenalin rush, no 'butterflies'. It felt like just another race. The other competitors were way too fast, and after the race I decided that I would never again feel so dispirited. The race that you have trained so long and hard for needs to be the pinnacle moment and, no matter in which position you finish, the reward is that you have done your very best.

Kieran surprised himself by picking up bronze medals in the men's 100 m and 200 m backstroke (B3 for the visually impaired), his first Paralympic medals and the beginning of a medal swag that would ultimately follow.

I was happy with the javelin event where I finished a creditable fourth. I had clearly improved, but was having second thoughts. I just knew that I was never going to get the big distances. I couldn't get the timing right, even after years of coaching. My body type was changing. It wasn't suited to swimming and I decided to let javelin go too. I knew that whatever sport I chose next, I would have to start at the bottom – but I always enjoy a challenge.

Cycling was introduced as a sport at the 1988 Seoul Paralympics; tandem road bike racing started in 1992 at Barcelona. I watched these events fascinated and impressed, and checked to see that my vision met the eligibility standards.

To be allowed to ride tandem behind a sighted pilot, a para-athlete may have any level of visual impairment between no light perception in either eye through to a visual acuity of 6/60 – or a visual field of less than 20°.

My degree of vision impairment clearly met the criteria. I'd always enjoyed bikes and cycling, and the speed that the tandems generated in their road race was exciting. At the end of the Games, it is customary to exchange some of your nationally badged clothing with members of other teams. I swapped a pair of my shorts for a pair of Canadian knicks, or bike shorts – my first cycling clothes, and all in red and white maple leaves!

Many years before, Kieran had ridden on a tandem bike on South Australian roads. Peggy (Scott) Bell believes that she had planted this seed of interest in him when he was only 11 years old:

> I like to feel that his love of bike riding started at Townsend cottage. On weekends, Kieran and I would often go for long bike rides, many times into Adelaide. When his older brother Mark came to stay for the weekend, he would come along too. On one occasion, when Kieran was 13, I needed to visit my mum in McLaren Vale Hospital (about 35 km south of Adelaide) and having three boys with me, I put a tandem (our cottage tandem was more like a toy bike with 24-inch wheels, 3-speed gears, two big fat saddles and a pack rack on the back) and a normal bike in the van so that they could ride home when they got bored. After greeting my mum, Kieran and Mark jumped on the tandem and Aaron took the single bike. After the visit, I began the drive back to Adelaide looking out for the boys. I picked up Aaron just out of McLaren Vale and then set out to collect the tandem – but they beat me home! Mark told me later how determined they were to win the race. Kieran was whooping it up as they passed cars coming down the long and steep Cement Hill descent where the speed limit was 60 kph!

Tandem bike racing was not new to international sport. It had simply been reintroduced in 1992. The 2000 m tandem cycling event had been a long-time inclusion in the Olympic cycling program and was held for men in 1906, 1908, 1920, then at all following Olympiads including 1972. In the early days, the tandem cyclists were given a time limit of four minutes, with the winner being the leader when the time was up.

From this format, it developed into a 2000 m sprint.

Tandem cycling gave Australia one of the most bizarre gold medals in its Olympic history. Before the 1952 Helsinki Olympic Games, the Australian Lionel Cox had never even been on a tandem. His countryman Russell Mockridge had some experience, but the two only ended up in the event because Mockridge had been given the tandem bike after the British Olympic team had decided it had no use for it. The first hurdle the pair had to overcome was to assemble the bike. Once they had achieved that minor feat, they had to figure out how to work as a team. They were fast learners. Mockridge and Cox improved in every round and against all odds, finished as gold medallists in the event.

In the early days of tandem racing they often raced on outdoor 330 m (or even longer) tracks. The creation of, and move toward, the indoor 250 m wooden board velodromes led to many crashes and accidents. Sprint cycling used to be ruthless, with fewer rules, and so cutting off, pushing, elbowing and even headbutting (where possible) were all useful tactics. Tandem racing just became too dangerous. In a real sense the reintroduction of tandems in the Paralympics has shown that with bikes ridden well and skilfully, tandem racing can be safe, even when a member of the team is vision impaired.

Again, I sought out my former coach, John Hamann, to talk about my sporting future.

John recounts this meeting:

> It was no surprise to me when Kieran swam fast enough to qualify for the Barcelona Games. Barcelona was quite a thrill for him, but swimming was always just going to be a stepping stone back to athletics for Kieran. When he came to see me to tell me he was getting tired of swimming the black line lap after lap and that he wanted to try something different, I was

> in complete agreement with him. He tried the javelin for a while, but found that his elbow was still not right, so I told him to buy a bike and suggested that he ride with his sister Tania. He was strong and powerful enough to ride as well as any cyclist and I was sure that Tania would push him for some time. He enjoyed riding and had said many times how the thrill of riding fast, especially downhill, excited him.

After the Barcelona Paralympics, my parents hired a car and we toured Europe together. For part of that time we stayed with a friend, Alfons Frenkl, in Ralbitz-Rosenthal, a municipality in the district of Bautzen in eastern Saxony (a federal state of Germany). This was a predominantly Sorbish area and Alfons, a schoolteacher, was teaching this language. I was fascinated to learn of my Wendish/Sorbish heritage.

On returning to Australia, I was faced with the reality of finding a job. Once I began to realise the complications of my medical condition, it became more obvious that I couldn't be a farmer or return to the home farm. I also realised that I didn't have the work ethic that my brothers had. When I was home I loved the farm environment, but I also took lots of rests. I remember Dad telling me: 'Find a job, son. Don't pay too much attention to these Paralympics. They won't get you anywhere!'

Deciding to follow Dad's advice, I enrolled in a degree course in Recreation and Planning Management, and began at the Salisbury campus near Adelaide, but finished at The Levels campus after Salisbury closed. I found studying and this course a challenge and took four years to complete a three-year course.

I had also met a girl, Kerry Golding – or, to be more accurate, she met me. We shared a mutual friend, Heidi Meakins. Heidi's sister, Susie, was one of Kerry's best friends at school. A year earlier,

Susie, Kerry and I had spent an evening together at the Pancake Kitchen in Adelaide. My abiding memory of that event was of the maple syrup. I love it and managed to finish a whole bottle on my stack of three pancakes.

Fortunately, Kerry's abiding memory of the Pancake Kitchen was me. Thankfully she wanted to spend more time with me, but was very shy. Kerry's older sister Sharyn decided to act. She found out my phone number and using Kerry's phone sent me a text message. Assuming it was from Kerry, I responded and a relationship was born. It blossomed quickly, once again helped by my love of food and eating. I was living at Gilles Plains and Kerry was staying at Christies Beach, about an hour away. Kerry would drive over and bring me dinner. I was not good at cooking for myself. I got by on lollies, Weet-Bix and powdered milk. So, I was really impressed with Kerry ... and her cooking!

When they met, Kerry was completing a Community Service Course at the Noarlunga TAFE (Technical and Further Education) with the aim of working in child or aged care. Born in Nowra, a city near the coast in New South Wales approximately 160 km south of Sydney, her family moved to Adelaide when her father, Chris, left the Navy to train as a policeman. His first posting was Clare in a pretty, grape-growing valley 140 km north of Adelaide

Soon after meeting Kerry, I moved into a house in Croydon with my sister Tania and brother Darren. Riding a bike was my chief mode of transport and I decided to join a cycling club. My first attempt wasn't successful. I told the club I was vision impaired and, after some deliberation, they refused to let me join. Undeterred, I approached another club – the Kilkenny Cycling Club. This time I raced at the club's track before telling them I was vision impaired.

They were so impressed, that when I then told them about my vision problems, they said: 'All you've got to do is watch the back wheel of the rider in front of you!' I was hooked.

There was also some disappointment at the time, as John Hamann recalls:

> He joined the Kilkenny Cycling Club and rode with its many members. At first he kept quiet about his poor vision but gradually it became known and a few of his mates rode to protect him as they fostered his talent as a cyclist. After he started racing in the velodrome, the concern for his and other cyclists' safety came to a head and he was forbidden to ride with his teammates in certain races. This ruling really upset him and concerned us. However, we could do little about it, except get him onto a tandem bike.

At Kilkenny, Kieran moved quickly through D and C to B grade. Those who have watched cycling know how quickly the bikes move and how close the cyclists are to each other. One mistake can bring down many other riders.

My new cycling club mates were surprised at how well I rode and were often curious to know what I could actually see. I told them that I can see enough shapes not to crash, but my reaction time must be a lot faster than that of a sighted rider, because I can't see anything in the distance. When I recognise a shape, it is suddenly in front of me, so I need to react like lightning. I'm okay when other riders are all around me. I can feel them, hear them, vaguely see their shapes and I just hammer along as fast as I can (and sometimes manage to beat them). It's a different story if I get left behind and the pack disappears into the distance and I can't see them anymore. So I learnt very quickly to keep up. Sometimes when I'm not sure where the others are I just get in front and go full pelt for the line. I rode single bikes for about seven years and was proud that in that time I wasn't involved in a single accident. I didn't cause any, nor did I crash into or hurt anyone.

My cycling group had an interesting nickname for me. When the cyclists ventured off the track and into the hilly countryside, I loved it and my energy levels seemed to rise. When the going got tough, I would ride from one struggling rider to the next, placing my hand on their backs and pushing them along. My fellow riders called me the 'Hand of God'.

In 2014 I met Maria Smith, the then membership director of the Norwood Cycling Club and the first club Kieran approached. With a smile on her face and tongue firmly planted in her cheek, she made the following offer:

> If and when Kilkenny Club folds and Kieran wants to come back to his roots, he can come back to Norwood and I'll even waive his transfer fee.

In para-swimming events Kieran's vision impairment was classified as B3, which meant he only raced against other B3 athletes. In tandem cycling, all three levels in B ride against each other. The B represents vision impairment. Within the Bs are three sub-groups. B1 is for athletes who are totally blind. B2 and B3 are for athletes who have limited vision in both eyes either in visual acuity (how far they can see) or visual field (how wide). The B2 and B3 vision requirements are subject to change. The most recent requirement for a B2 classification is 2/60 vision and tunnel vision less than 10° wide. For the B3s it is 6/60 vision and tunnel vision less than 40° wide – Kieran's category.

A position on a trip to the 1995 World Para-cycling Track Championships in Augsburg, Germany, became available and it was offered to Kieran. He raced with pilot Eddie Hollands in the B (sometimes called B1-3) Tandem Kilometre (better known as the Kilo). The Kilo begins with a standing start and athletes compete against the clock to complete the kilometre in the fastest time.

It was a good experience, but a bit scary too because my handlebars came loose during the Kilo. We didn't win, but while I was there I saw mixed tandem – males and females – riding together.

While I was away, Darren and Tania had moved out of their Croydon rental home, so when I got back I had nowhere to live. Kerry's parents offered me board. Kerry was a good netballer and liked sport. I liked her. She seemed to like me. The penny dropped and I asked her if she would be my sighted tandem bike pilot.

But Kerry had no previous experience with cycling and we didn't have a coach – or even a tandem bike! We found someone who had one and asked if we could borrow the frame. To this I bought and added the wheels and the rest of the equipment. There were many breakdowns, but we persisted, even though we had no real knowledge about how to become competitive. At this stage, we were the only tandem riders in South Australia and therefore truly pioneering this sport. Swimming and athletics are sports which one takes on mostly as an individual, whereas tandem cycling is all about teamwork. Kerry added an external motivation and driving force and helped me work and train even harder. We trained mostly alone at the Edwardstown outdoor cycling track. When we found out what times we needed to match or beat we tried to replicate them. But we were on an outdoor bituminised track and coping with outdoor weather conditions, especially wind.

Kerry needed to learn a lot and quickly, so with me as her coach, she rode a single bike to work and took every possible chance to improve. However, I hadn't been coached for cycling. I had been to the AIS and two Paralympic Games already by this time, so I thought I knew how to train. In those days, I believed that the only way to train to be a cyclist was to ride hard. We would often get up at 4 am and ride into the hills around Clarendon so that Kerry could get home to be ready for her shift at the local childcare centre by 6 am. It was always dark when we trained and the lights on the bikes were nearly useless. But thankfully there was little traffic at that time in the morning.

Training together had its moments. Kerry remembers well some of the early difficulties:

> We often trained on single bikes. Kieran would ride to the top of a hill quite quickly and then come back down to meet me struggling along. He would offer to help, but there was no way I wanted the 'Hand of God'! Under the pressure of training together on the tandem bike we would often have arguments. But we always left them with the bike. Kieran couldn't read the figures on our bike's cyclometer, so he constantly wanted to know how fast we were going, had we beaten the previous best time, how far had we ridden. I often felt that Kieran didn't trust my ability as a pilot, which was understandable because I had not ridden before and Kieran had taught me how to ride the way he rode. So, he was always advising me, over and over, and always right next to my ear. I can remember being in tears around the middle of a steep hill. I wanted to get off but Kieran kept hammering at me to keep going. It was so hard. Sometimes I would get so cross that I would get Kieran to pilot me so I could boss him around! This prompted Kieran to tell one of his favourite jokes.

A tandem rider is stopped by a police car.

'What've I done, officer?' asks the rider.

'Perhaps you didn't notice, sir, but your female friend fell off your bike a kilometre back ...'

'Oh, thank goodness for that,' says the rider – 'I thought I'd gone deaf!'

I'm not sure whether Kieran is teasing me when he tells this joke, so I usually remind him of another funny story.

A man and his wife were out riding on a tandem. As is mostly the case, the man is on the front seat and controlling the bike and says, 'Darling, do you think you could pedal a bit harder? I'm doing nearly all of the work.' And shortly afterwards: 'Darling, when we lean into corners, could you lean with me? By being tense, you are making it hard for me to steer.' A little further on and it's: 'Darling, could you avoid touching my back? You're hot and it makes me uncomfortable.'

The wife says, 'Darling, could you please stop the bike.' She gets off and turns her seat in the opposite direction. Flabbergasted he asks, 'Darling, what are you doing?' She replies, 'I'm going home ... ***darling***!'

To become eligible to ride in the fast-approaching Paralympics, we needed to prove to selectors that we would be competitive. This process began by racing together successfully with our club, Kilkenny. Success at this level led to selection into the Atlanta training squad chosen by the Australian Paralympics Federation (APF), supervised by Ken Norris. There were only nine tandem team places available. Could we win one of these and be on the plane to America?

We hoped to put that issue to rest at a Perth invitation meet in March. Together we won the Kilo, establishing a new world record time of 1:14.3. We also won the 11.3 km road time trial and the 50 km road race, the 3000 m pursuit, the 200 m fly and the criterium. This particular criterium included 30 minutes of tactical riding, where anyone lapped was eliminated from the race. After the half hour was up, those left had a two-lap sprint to determine the winner. Although we had won all the events entered at the meet, we still waited anxiously for the official announcement of the Atlanta Paralympic squad.

Kieran: I am enjoying our conversations, but why are you putting them at the end of each chapter?

Uncle Andy: *It's kind of Brechtian, isn't it? Bertolt Brecht was a German playwright who didn't want the audience to identify so completely with the actors that they became complacent. He wanted the audience to self-reflect and be moved to change opinions and perspectives – and then effect change in the world outside the theatre.*

So how did Brecht do that?

Well, during some of his plays the actor would directly address the audience or might sing a song to interrupt the action. He used harsh and bright stage lighting to keep the audience alert, and explanatory placards or the ploy of speaking the stage directions out loud. He used any strategy that would remind the audience that the play was a representation of reality *and not reality itself.*

Why did you want to do this in the book?

I think that it is easy to lose oneself in your story, Kieran. Kerry and you are doing incredible things in the story – so impressive that I think the reader will forget that you have only 15% sight. I want to remind the reader of this. I would like to put this as a postscript on each chapter – like one of Brecht's placards: DON'T FORGET THAT THIS GUY IS 85% BLIND!

But how will that help?

As I've talked to you and Kerry, I've come to appreciate some of the difficulties visually impaired people face. I will never understand completely because I can see, but I want our readers and the community to recognise the courage and resilience of people like you. The way you have gone about your life is inspirational.

But my life is not a play or a drama. I've just tackled life and the problems of visual impairment as they've arisen.

I've always believed that true champions are generally humble and you fit that description. I hope that in reading your story, sighted people like myself will become more tolerant and understanding ... that reading this book helps.

That would be a wonderful outcome.

5 Atlanta and the hole in the leg

1996–1999

Only six months after Kerry had agreed to become my tandem pilot, we were chosen to represent Australia at the 1996 Atlanta Paralympics in the USA. Our two events were to be the B Mixed Tandem Kilometre and the B Mixed Tandem Sprint.

Paralympic cyclists compete under the same rules and conditions as their counterparts at the Olympic Games. The weather in Atlanta was typically hot and very humid. Just outside the velodrome, spectators were treated to fog machines to keep them cool. Once inside the open-air venue, cyclists and spectators were at the mercy of semi-tropical conditions and did all they could to hydrate and stay cool. It was going to be hot work, but the Aussie pair was flying and in the lead-up to the Games had broken the world record in the Kilo. They were the clear favourites. It was all going so well, until disaster struck!

While practising the day before the event, Kieran and Kerry crashed badly. It is important to remember that track bikes don't have brakes, but Kerry is quick to acknowledge her inexperience:

> It was my fault that we came down so heavily. Our back tyre blew and I came down the track too quickly. I had no idea how to handle this and the bike just gathered more speed. When we crashed at the bottom, Kieran's handlebar dug into my left thigh. I've still got the hole where it got stuck inside the muscle.

But it wasn't all Kerry's fault. I had a part to play in that crash too. We didn't have mechanics in those days and I had fitted the rear tyre, the one that blew. I just hadn't been careful enough. The bike was fishtailing and hard to control, but we might have got out of this better by riding further up the track and slowing the bike down gradually.

The initial diagnosis of Kerry's injury at the track was a fractured leg, so she was transferred immediately to the local hospital. Scans and X-rays revealed extensive bruising to the quads, and a split muscle.

I was prepared to call a halt to our Atlanta campaign. We were a team, but it was Kerry who was hurting. We now knew that the leg wasn't broken, but it was in a very bad way. I was fully prepared to stop, but Kerry insisted that we continue with the dream. She said, 'We've done all this work. We've come all this way. We're not going to let this beat us.' She is an amazing girl with incredible courage.

The only cure for Kerry was to rest, ice and elevate the leg, and administer codeine. Codeine was chosen to relieve the pain because of the rules about banned substances. I was up all night icing the leg because we were due to race our favoured one kilometre event the next day.

For the rest of the Games Kerry was confined to a wheelchair and had to be lifted on and off the bike. The muscle had seized up and Kerry had to work agonisingly hard to get even one revolution of the pedals. She kept going forwards and backwards, stretching a bit further each time until she could do it.

When we got the bike going and the race came around, I was tentative about how much power I could put down. I didn't know what Kerry could handle and clearly didn't want another crash. We came sixth in the Kilometre. We should have won it. We had just broken the world record. But under the circumstances it was a good result because Kerry's leg was now moving.

In the Tandem Sprint, the first round is a 200 m time trial, with the eight fastest pairs progressing to the knockout stages. The event then becomes a head-to-head knockout in a best of three contest, usually over three laps (however this depends on the size of the velodrome and can range from 600 m to 1000 m). The sprint is a highly tactical 'cat and mouse' event, with riders jockeying for position before committing themselves to sprint for the line.

An understanding of drafting or slipstreaming is integral to cycling. A cyclist moving forward creates turbulent waves called vortices, or low-pressure areas, behind them. For the cyclists following, these low-pressure areas suck you forward while eddies push you forward. The lead rider gets a small advantage if trailed, because the rider behind reduces the leader's turbulence. In wind tunnel tests, where four cyclists are racing quickly and in line (four-man pace line), the lead rider expended about 97% energy. The second rider used about 71% and the next two 65% energy. It makes a lot of sense to draft whenever possible.

On the same afternoon of our Kilo disappointment, we rode the '200 metre fly' used to seed the sprints. Riders are given four laps to build up speed and are timed over the last 200 m. Understandably we were one of the slowest qualifiers, forcing us to ride against the fastest qualifiers the following day.

Seeded against the new favourites, we looked to have missed out when we lost to the Italian pair Manuela Agnese and Damiano Zanotti. But our competitive times kept us in contention. Now we had to beat two British riders in the repechage event to stay in the competition, and we did.

Kerry's leg was moving more freely, but the muscle was still bleeding internally. She was learning how to tolerate the pain and what she could do. The races from then on were best of three. Because of Kerry's leg we needed to win in two. Our coach was terrific. He had watched the other teams and told us the best way to beat our opposition. The reality was that we didn't have a lot of choice. We couldn't accelerate quickly and so we ground down our opposition over the distance. We had to treat each race just like the Kilo time trial. It wasn't really 'cat and mouse' – more like 'the hare and the tortoise'.

By now the pair was the subject of much public attention. The other competitors and crowds watched as Kerry was wheel-chaired into the velodrome and lifted on to the tandem. She would finish races with tears of pain streaming down her face and then cycle slowly around the pits (the central area of the velodrome) until her next race to prevent the leg from seizing up. Meanwhile the other riders were heading off for refreshing showers, ice baths and massages. Everyone was waiting to see when, rather than if, Kerry would crack. What the others didn't know was that the doctors had made it very clear to the pair that if the internal bleeding reached the knee it would 'lock up', the pain would be unbearable and they would be withdrawn from racing. Kerry wasn't enjoying the pain or being confined to a wheelchair:

> Our coach thought he would put my pain in perspective and said, 'This won't be worse than having a baby!' All that did was nearly put me off ever having children. I hated being in a wheelchair. Everyone kept telling me, 'Kerry, look around you. Every second person here needs to use a wheelchair!'

We needed to overcome the top-ranked Americans Scott Evans and Clara Dunn in the best of three semi-finals, which we did in straight sets. To win the gold medal we were up against our nemesis of the previous day, the Italian duo. I was very worried about the pain Kerry was enduring. We knew that we were assured of a silver medal even if we withdrew from the gold medal ride-off. I told the coaches that I was ready to quit and settle for silver just to put an end to Kerry's suffering.

Kerry was having none of this but can't recall much of what happened next:

> A lot of those races are a bit of a blur. I can remember the power coming through the bike. When Kieran gets going you can feel this surge of power. It's often quite difficult to hold the bike steady. When our final race came around, I don't think we fully realised that we were riding for gold. We were just taking it one race at a time. I remember yelling and screaming out there. I kept telling Kieran to go faster, go faster, and that seemed to work well. It was a bit of a shock when we won and it took some time for it to sink in. We did over ten match sprint races in two days to get that precious gold medal!

Kieran and Kerry had won gold for Australia in the B Tandem Sprint. As their dramatic campaign unfolded it had gripped the imagination of the entire velodrome. Even the impartial UCI officials were joining in with the crowd applause by the time the final arrived. The Commissar of the meet, Britain's Barry Broadbent, said he had never seen anything like it. The story of Kerry's courage filtered back into Australian newspapers. Kerry's Atlanta campaign was over and Kieran was given permission to ride in his remaining road events with a new pilot, Sandra Smith from Perth. But he felt satisfaction in what he had achieved with Kerry and was also aware of the difficulty in forming a new partnership with so little time for preparation. Kieran decided that it was Kerry or no one and so abandoned the road races.

With gold medals hanging around their necks and showing all the signs of being in love, Kieran and Kerry were often asked if they were engaged. Kieran would always answer with a grin, 'Maybe?'

After the Games, we travelled around America with Mum and Dad. Once Kerry stopped the racing and the exercising, her leg injury healed quite quickly. We travelled up to Vancouver to stay with Kerry's Uncle John. In an era before mobile phone technology, Kerry had tried in numerous phone boxes en route to contact her parents in Australia. The evening before we arrived at John's home, Mum, Dad and I were alarmed to hear cries of anguish coming from a telephone box.

Sylvia remembers the distress:

> We were shocked to realise that it was Kerry. She went into the telephone box and then we heard her crying and screaming. Kieran went to console her. While Kerry had been travelling around America and Canada, her much-loved grandfather had died. Her family had decided not to tell her until she returned to Australia, but had realised that Uncle John knew about the death and it wasn't right that she should hear the bad news from him.

It took some time for Kerry to come to terms with her loss. She was grieving; and angry and upset that the sad news had been kept from her:

> I can now understand why my parents made the decision to tell me later. I loved my grandfather dearly. I would have packed my bags and left Atlanta immediately to return to Australia if they had told me sooner. It would have meant that our effort to win gold for Australia would have resulted in nought.

Dad and Mum left Vancouver to return to Australia. We stayed on. I had planned a surprise! We took our bikes on a ferry ride to

Vancouver Island. We rode around a bit and there on the beach I proposed to Kerry.

Kerry accepted Kieran's proposal, but adds mischievously:

> Kieran had planned it. He had the ring. He was just waiting to see if I could help him win a gold medal!

Attached to the ring was a heart Kieran bought in Vancouver and a selection of trinkets he had collected on their trip, so he had clearly been planning the proposal for some time.

When asked to recall my most memorable sporting event, my choice is this first gold medal in Atlanta. I am in awe of a person who could leave a hospital bed and endure such pain to achieve a goal. There was nothing I could do but watch her bravery. What she put on the line to keep the team going was remarkable. It was such a memorable moment and just so wonderful to share it with someone I had fallen in love with.

The new Paralympic B Tandem Pursuit champions now had the home Sydney 2000 Paralympics on their radar. How successful could they be if they were both fully fit, with another four years to prepare? But before those games would be the excitement of their wedding.

One should not be surprised that Kieran and Kerry had found love. After all, the history of the tandem bike is inextricably linked with romance and courtship. Some historians credit the development of cycling to the need initially for males to travel more widely in search of love. The two-wheeled 'safety bicycle' configuration that we recognise today as a tandem showed up in the early 1890s and was often called a 'courting bike'. As it would be unthinkable in those days to make a lady look at the backside of her male companion, it was only proper to place her in front where she would have a better view. In early tandem designs the chauffeur behind would steer the bike through a linkage from the rear position.

In Australia, an odd two-seater bicycle had been invented by Hubert Opperman, a famous Australian distance cyclist. The 'Side by Side' bicycle, also known as a 'sociable' or more recently as a buddy bike, was also used extensively for courting. Unlike a tandem where the riders are in line with one another, here the riders were side by side. Two seats, two pedal hangers, and two handlebars were mounted on either side of a frame made of steel tubing. The handlebars were linked so that both riders turned them to steer the bicycle. For a short time, a well-known Australian cycle manufacturing company Malvern Star (started by cyclist Tom Finnigan in the Melbourne suburb of Malvern in 1902) produced these strange bicycles. One can only presume that superior balance and coordination were needed to ride that invention in any predictable direction.

Many with an inventive flair have experimented with tandems. The conventional tandem has both riders facing forwards and the pilot in front controlling the steering, braking and gears (when brakes and gears are used). On one side of the frame a chain connects the pilot's crankset to the stoker's (the rear rider) crankset. On the other side a chain connects the stoker's crankset to the rear drive cog. The cranksets are identical so that both riders pedal stroke in time. Family friends of Kieran, Peter and Erika Kaesler, have built their own version – a collapsible tandem that can be transported in a suitcase. More unusual though, is that Peter and Erika have set up their tandem so that the stoker (the rear rider) rides with her back to the pilot in a 'back to back tandem'. The major advantage of this set-up is that the rear-facing stoker gets to have a view other than the back of the pilot's head.

Erika (the stoker) keeps pilot Peter informed of traffic behind. Using hand signals, she can communicate with approaching drivers, sometimes getting their attention back on to driving their vehicles responsibly:

> I have probably witnessed more inattentive driving from my back seat than most. There is the increasing distraction of mobile phones and navigation devices, together with other diversions like music and radio selection, passenger interaction, hair grooming and makeup application, eating off the dashboard, dressing and arranging apparel while driving. A lot of drivers squint and I can only assume that they should be wearing their glasses.

Peter has constantly adapted this bike:

> A front and rear suspension was critical for the safety of the stoker as the stoker facing backwards could not see and anticipate the bumps coming. The connecting chain drive between the riders was reversed for the rear rider by a figure 8 chain – like a rearward-facing bike providing forward effort. Because of the tandem suspension, the bike developed an oscillation when our pedals were synchronised – and we bounced in a wave-like motion as we rode along. To combat this, we offset the pedals at 90° and this countered the oscillation effect. Now when one rider's pedals are at the top and bottom of the stroke (generating no power) the other rider is in the power zone. Another positive result of offsetting the pedals was that taking off was much smoother. The downside was that standing on the pedals to go uphill became difficult as we were out of sync. Changes in the future will be a set of front forks with suspension lock out. Riding downhill and turning at speed over slight bumps can be dangerous as the active suspension inhibits positive steering.

On a recent trip to Europe the pair discovered that their tandem was not only a means of transport, but also a talking point and a way to meet many people along the way. They were stopped about five or six times a day for photos.

Peter noticed too that they were able to keep up with the solo riders:

> We were definitely slower going up the hills; however, tandem riding is all about the downhill experience if you can hang on. After being passed by conventional bike riders on the hills, we gained on the downhill so we were constantly passing each other.

The year finished well for Kieran and Kerry. In late 1996 Kieran was honoured as the winner of ABC Radio stations 5CK and 5LN Sports Achiever Award and then, on the following Australia Day, both were delighted to be told that they were the recipients of a Medal of the Order of Australia and certificate (OAM) for services to sport. The medals were presented to Kieran and Kerry the following April by the South Australian Governor, Sir Eric Neal.

In January 1997, Kieran was invited to open the Tunarama festival in Port Lincoln. Held over the Australia Day weekend, Tunarama is a festival celebration of the local fishing industry. Kieran's home town's newspaper, the Lincoln Times, *had kept residents updated on his athletic career, and not just content to attend Tunarama as a tourist or spectator, Kieran entered the weekend cycling event and triathlon. As a novelty, competitors could team up for the triathlon, so one team member would swim, another cycle and the third member run. Understandably Kieran was asked to be the cycling member in these teams and over three years and six races, he was a member of the winning team four times and came second twice.*

Two months later I was honoured to be asked to open the Little Athletics Regional Championship in Port Lincoln and to demonstrate to the attending children and parents the technique of javelin and discus throwing and the correct way to push the shot put.

Planning our wedding led to many spirited debates. Originally, we settled on an October wedding, but then decided on May because it was off-peak season for weddings and would save money. However, May is not an 'off-season' for farmers. The grain growers are busy seeding and many of my family are involved with agriculture. We also had differing opinions about where we would spend our honeymoon. Kerry wanted to spend a week in Tasmania, but I didn't want to spend that sort of money.

Wedding day, 3 May, came and we awoke to rain that marked the end of a long dry spell. With the farmers happy about that and unable to work, the wedding day went off perfectly. We were married by Pastor Paul Fielke in St Stephens Lutheran Church in Adelaide and then finished our magical day at a reception at the Clarendon Winery.

Kerry won the honeymoon debate. We flew to Tasmania, hired a car and travelled almost right around the island state. Dad's sister Erica was living in Legana, a pretty town on the Tamar River near Launceston, and we enjoyed catching up with her on our circuit.

When we returned to South Australia we continued to train hard and our times just kept getting better.

* * *

The 1998 Para-cycling Track World Championships were held in Colorado Springs, USA, a hilly city averaging 1828 m above sea level. Pikes Peak, part of the Southern Rocky Mountain range, is 4302 m high.

We were sent on a training run to the mountains nearby. The air was thinner and it was difficult to ride and breathe, but we needed to adjust. We noticed that our heart rates increased to get more oxygen flowing through our bodies. To add to her discomfort, Kerry had a bout of severe food poisoning and because she was vomiting between races, the gossip was that she was pregnant. The German doctors offered Kerry tablets, but the rumours about them having all sorts of performance-enhancing drugs abounded, so we were reluctant. We checked with our Australian coach and he approved. So Kerry took the German tablets and they helped enormously. Because she was so sick, we asked the Americans if we could defer our race till the next day, but this was the team we had beaten in Atlanta and they declined our request. That made us even more determined to win the event.

The biggest obstacle to a cyclist is not friction on the ground, but pushing the air. Here the air was thinner so we rode very fast, taking ten seconds off our personal best time in the 3000 m Pursuit.

They were not the only athletes to do personal best times in Colorado Springs. Amazingly, the world record before this meet was bettered by nine teams at these championships. The last of these were the German pair of Michaela Fuchs and Jan Ratzke. Kerry was determined to reclaim that record time:

> When we saw the Germans break the record, it revved us up a bit because they were a hundredth of a second faster than us for the 200 m fly. We really wanted that 200 m record. When they broke the world Kilo time we said, 'You're not going to get this one too!' It was exhilarating to win the race and set a world record.

The 1998 World Championships was one of our most successful meets and we won all the events we entered – the B Mixed Tandem

Sprint, Pursuit, Kilo (both in world record time) and, finally, the Time Trials.

Australia Day in 1999 began with a breakfast at Government House in the presence of His Excellency Sir Eric Neal, AC. After the meal, the Governor presented Kieran with The Premier's Award for Outstanding Community Service, adding that it was not for Kieran's sporting achievements, but for his work with children who are blind and those underprivileged.

Cycling success continued at the 1999 European Championships in Blois, France. Kerry remembers the condition of the track:

> When we arrived we were surprised to see people still working on the track. It was outdoors and in very poor condition. The surface was cracked, bumpy and had weeds growing out of it. I got the nickname 'Token Chick' from the riders from other countries. I was the only female in a very large Australian team.

If the track wasn't bad enough, we were presented with other challenges. I remember the intense rivalry. After our qualifying race the mechanics deflated our tyres so they wouldn't expand in the sun. When we got on the track to race again, it was hard to get the bike going. The back felt spongy and was bouncing around. At first, we thought it was due to the bad track surface, but then we realised what our problem was – the mechanics had forgotten to reinflate our rear tyre! We lost the race.

In the sprints, we were up against the Germans. They had their male cyclist on the front and their vision-impaired female athlete on the back. I could see the big, strong German male eyeballing Kerry and trying to intimidate her. He didn't look back at me. He probably thought he was about to have an easy win. It turned out to be a tough race and they rode so close to us that their pilot's pedal took the skin off Kerry's ankle. That got Kerry really excited and we won. After the race and somewhat ironically, the Germans protested, but the German doctors who saw what had happened couldn't do enough for us.

It was at the Blois Velodrome 30 years earlier that one of the world's greatest riders, Eddy Merckx, came to grief in a derny race. A derny is a motorbike used for motor-paced cycling events. Interestingly, before the invention of the motorbike, tandems were sometimes used to pace events because of their superior speed capability. Merckx and close friend and derny driver Fernand Wambst usually worked brilliantly together, but at this event they crashed. Wambst was killed instantly and Merckx suffered a cracked vertebra and severely twisted pelvis. These wounds healed, but he was left with an imbalance that made cycling painful and difficult for the rest of his career.

This was the only time in my sporting career that I had a commercial sponsor – the Dairy Farmers – Oak Milk Company. They didn't pay us in money, but in milk, crates of it!

On the work front, I was teaching a cycling program with David Gomer at Morphett Vale High School between 1997 and 2000.

This school was one of four specialist sports schools. Under the State Government's Athlete Ambassador initiative, Kieran was employed 20 hours a week to work with Dave and the students. While he occasionally spoke to classes, most of his time was spent on bicycle maintenance and riding with students during practical lessons. Of the 90 Year 8 students who applied for entry to the program, only 20 were selected. This group not only had to train more intensively, but integrate their newfound knowledge of cycling into other school subjects like mathematics, science and English. Kieran enjoyed this five-day-a-week job and was disappointed when the funding ran out.

Six months out from the Sydney Games, Kerry gave up her job in childcare. The couple wanted to focus on the upcoming Paralympics and Kerry was often unwell:

> I loved working in childcare, but I must have a low tolerance to viruses and illnesses. It seemed that I would catch any sickness going around the centre. Another complication was that my shifts were continually changing and I was missing quite a lot of training and making it difficult for Kieran. We were okay financially, so I gave the job up to be 100% ready for Australia's home Paralympics.

Kerry was soon to have another reason to take a break from work:

> I was feeling really tired and saw a doctor to ask for iron pills. But he said that was not what was needed, that I was pregnant. I passed on the news to Kieran during a training ride. I just said to him, 'Are you ready to be a dad?' He said he was, but he looked very surprised. I told him that he had to lose weight so that I could put it on.

Kerry and Kieran didn't tell their coaches about the pregnancy fearing Kerry might be withdrawn from competition at the Sydney Paralympics. Was this a mistake? Would Kerry be fit enough? Would the baby be safe? The soon-to-be parents approached their next big championships with more questions than answers.

6 Sydney and the hex

2000–2003

The home Olympic Games in Sydney had been widely acclaimed and in a memorable valedictory, IOC President Juan Antonio Samaranch described them as 'the best games ever'. Australian athletes had excelled and a euphoric and patriotic Australian public were ready to enjoy Paralympic Games success.

About to start our family and with the Games organisers making it clear that there would be no mixed tandem event at the following Paralympics in Athens, we knew this was to be our last chance to ride together. We had trained conscientiously and were in great form. Leaving our South Australian coach, we went to the pre-Games training camp in Perth, Western Australia, and were told that in our current form, we were almost sure to succeed.

They hadn't told Kevin McIntosh, the Australian coach, about the pregnancy, but Kevin had worked it out for himself. When asked by the media about the pregnancy, Kevin gave the reporters a positive spin:

> I sort of picked it. Kerry and Kieran started showing maternal and paternal instincts. Coaches just know these things. It is great news. Kerry has been as good as she's ever been and their times are certainly right up there.

Nevertheless, away from the media Kevin was annoyed to be informed so close to the Games and he was concerned about the risks:

> Kieran turned up to training camp and I hadn't seen him for a while. Prior to that training camp, he had ducked and weaved from me. It got to the point where he was told that if he didn't attend the training camp, he wasn't going to the Games. When he got to the camp it was obvious why he had been avoiding me – Kerry was pregnant and I should have been made aware of this much earlier. We were all surprised that the pregnancy was so advanced and it became a case of risk management, as tandem cycling is a dangerous sport. I talked to them both many times about the risks. Kieran clearly wanted to ride with Kerry in Sydney and he was adamant that she wanted to ride too. It had been a goal of his for a long time.

Kerry had been assured that she could still ride safely during her pregnancy, but she was a little nervous when she first got back on the bike. It didn't take long for her to put aside those fears and the pair rode encouraging times.

But then things began to go awry. Although the Sydney coaches were annoyed at first to suddenly find Kerry four months pregnant, it was known that many athletes have had good experiences with pregnancies, some even performing better during this time. However, the new coaches worked their charges very hard.

Kerry didn't enjoy this new training regime:

> Training was just riding as hard as possible and this was what Perth and Sydney felt like. I think that's what blew away my interest in cycling in general. Every day my legs were tired. Every day I didn't feel good. The Perth pre-training camp went for a fortnight. It was constant and constantly hard. They knew that I was pregnant and I'm not sure that they'd had much experience with this. Pregnant athletes generally need more recovery time. We felt we were riding too far. Sometimes we feigned an injury just to have a break in the support car.

Our sport was in a transitional stage. In Atlanta, we had had to do everything by and for ourselves, but significant money had been allocated to the Sydney campaign. The coaching personnel and mechanics were now highly credentialled professionals and we appreciated a significant improvement in equipment. We were open to any suggestions about new structures and training regimes because we believed it would improve our performance. Perhaps we followed the advice too closely. In retrospect, we both felt that we were over-trained.

At the pre-training camp we were just humming along. But the experts thought we could be even quicker if we changed our warm-up strategy. They wanted us to warm up harder and so we followed this advice. But when it came to the race, I felt tired. The tapering-off period between the camp and the Games was too short for me. On race day, I felt I had lost a quarter of my energy.

To make matters worse, we had to borrow a road bike! We flew our bikes all over the world, but between Perth and Sydney our $6000 road tandem bike got destroyed. Our bike was being put on a carrier and when taking it off the plane through a doorway, they bent the back end of the bike at a 45° angle. The airline was a sponsor of the Sydney Paralympic Games! The replacement tandem had not been specially set up for our body types and was uncomfortable.

I owned that bike and Dad thought that with the help of a specialist TIG (Tungsten Inert Gas) welder he could fix the tandem. However, time was critical and the bike needed to be assessed by the insurers first. It all proved to be too difficult and the airline went into receivership before I could claim compensation. Dad eventually took the bike back to Port Lincoln and fixed it himself.

We were given newly designed helmets. I couldn't hear anything except the roar of the crowd and certainly couldn't hear the lap numbers being called out. The Australian head coach was standing near the official lap caller and he couldn't hear him either. The helmet was like a drum and amplified the crowd noise, which in Sydney was far louder than we had ever experienced. Kerry couldn't hear the lap caller, but at least she could see the lap board. The new helmets were cleverly designed to lower wind resistance, but I missed the wind on my face. I enjoy speed and the rushing wind helps to get my adrenalin pumping. We finished a disappointing fifth in our favourite 3000 m Pursuit, only missing out on a medal ride-off by a fraction of a second. In the Kilo we managed another fifth, but we were now well off the pace. Our time of 1:11.603 for the kilometre was blitzed by the winner Pamela Fernandes of the USA with a world record of 1:08.997.

To compound their problems, Kerry was sick again:

> I think I am more susceptible to food poisoning than most. Perhaps it is the way a food hall works, but in Sydney I was sick again and needed medication to stop the vomiting.

When it came to their sprint event, the combination of all of this and especially Kerry's pregnancy caused her to faint due to low blood pressure after losing their quarter final:

> I got off the bike. I knew I was in trouble. Kieran and Kevin, my coach, grabbed me on my way down. I was devastated. My parents were in the crowd. They had never seen us race before and I so wanted them to see us up on that dais with medals around our necks and everyone singing our national anthem. We were the record holders and the champions. We expected to win and we wanted to be able to tell our baby that she had won a medal with us at the 2000 Sydney Paralympics.

Kerry had fainted because her blood supply pooled in her legs and uterus, depriving her brain of oxygen. The defence mechanism kicked in and looked after the baby first. Kerry had ultrasounds to check the baby's condition and everything was okay, but her Sydney Paralympic dream was over.

Their coach, Kevin was also devastated:

> Kerry was struggling and the officials questioned me about this. I should have withdrawn them. I looked at Kerry and she said she was fine, but I knew she wasn't. We all knew something was wrong, because when Kieran and Kerry were slowing down after their race, their tandem began to weave and wobble. They managed to get it down on to the flat and then the bike and riders fell in a heap onto the concrete as Kerry fainted. If something had happened to her and/or the baby, I would have carried that pain for the rest of my life. Being a father myself, I knew then and there that I would never put myself into that situation again. Allowing them to ride was the first mistake I made as a coach. It's something I will always carry and it changed the way I worked. I tended to listen too much to what the athletes said. I have a great passion for the man ... and for Kerry. I think they are great people. They were absolutely committed to what they were doing, but she shouldn't have raced. We discovered the pregnancy too close to the Games and we couldn't change the team. If Kerry hadn't got pregnant they would have won gold. They would have won even if she was three months less pregnant.

My sister, Tania, piloted me in the road races, but that didn't have a happy ending either.

Road events are contested over varying numbers of laps of a closed road circuit ranging from 6 to 15 km in distance. There are two alternatives – the road race and the time trial. In the road race, riders begin with a bunched start and the first riders to cross the finishing line win. In the time trial, competitors start at 60-second intervals and the riders completing the distance in the shortest time are declared the winners.

We were doing very well in our road race until we had mechanical problems and kept slipping the chain that connects the riders. The mechanics had shifted all the gear from my broken frame (thanks to poor cargo handling) on to another frame and hadn't stretched the brand-new chain put on just before the race began. Stopping three times to replace the chain, we finished a creditable seventh – less than four minutes behind the winners.

I have nothing but praise for Kerry and Tania. They are both terrific pilots with contrasting styles. Tania is more aggressive with her steering and more likely to go more directly for a corner. At times her aggression terrified me and I put it down to her experience on motorbikes. I remember that when Tania worked at Telstra she overheard some male friends bragging about their motorbike riding skills. When she told them that she rode motorbikes too, they scoffed. Tania challenged them to prove their superiority. They later met at the Mallala racetrack where the boys had set up a slalom course, a series of cones that had to be negotiated in the quickest time possible. Tania, with her farm riding experience, whipped them!

So, my experience of riding on home soil with Kerry and Tania to large adoring crowds ended with disappointment. We spent a lot of time trying to talk through stuff and trying to put everything behind us. But it was hard. Our confidence had been knocked around. Before, our focus had been sharp and we knew where we were going; now we were unsure. The main thing was Kerry's health and the baby. It is easy to win happily, but to lose graciously is a real art. We were very disappointed but we wanted to be gracious in defeat. Despite this, we now all look back on the event with positive attitudes and are appreciative of being there together.

Meanwhile Tania was enjoying cycling success with another partner. Back home together in Port Lincoln at Christmastime a few years before, Kieran had encouraged Tania to accompany him on long training rides. For a start, he took along a rope so that he could tow Tania when she got tired; however, his younger sister is a naturally gifted and determined sportsperson as well, and quickly improved her fitness. Evidence of Tania's sporting prowess is easy to find. In her student days at Port Lincoln High School and at their school sports days she excelled. Competing against students much older, Tania won all six events she entered and broke records in two of them.

Only 18 months before the Sydney Paralympics, I had talked Tania into being a pilot for a visually impaired cyclist. At the same time, I had convinced visually impaired South Australian Sarnya Parker to change from athletics to cycling. Opportunities were limited in athletics because disability categories were being cut.

Sarnya's account of Kieran's matchmaking goes like this:

> Kieran talked me into cycling. I was ranked fifth in the world as a Paralympic pentathlete, but I knew I wasn't improving enough to make Sydney. It was time for a tough decision. Kieran basically said, 'Sarnya, I've got just the perfect cycling partner for you.' And with that he introduced me to Tania, who took me for a ride and I said, 'Yeah, let's do it.'

The two girls hit it off and were a near perfect match. Tania had found the ideal tandem partner:

> From the very first time we rode together everyone said we rode so smoothly. We knew we were well matched. Our cadence was similar and we could read each other well. We worked at the same city office so we could cycle to and from our homes each day. And we got along – we never argued.

Despite Sarnya and Tania's lack of competitive cycling experience, they won two gold medals at the Sydney Paralympics in the women's open 1 km time trial tandem (the Kilo) and the women's open individual pursuit tandem, for which they both later received a Medal of the Order of Australia. In front of a roaring home crowd, Sarnya and Tania also broke the world record in both events. They were to continue their success together, winning another two gold medals at the 2001 European Championships held in Zurich, Switzerland.

I feel I have used the Sydney experience to good effect. I was very disappointed for Kerry. I wanted her to leave on a high. But I did learn some lessons from Sydney. I've learnt to listen to and take advice from many different sources. I take a bit from each of the coaches and pick out what suits me. I am far more independent now and confident of what it takes to be better. After the experience of seven Paralympic Games, the coaches trust me to know and carry this out.

After the Paralympics, Kieran received an Australian Sports Medal. This commemorative medal was a one-off awarded by the Governor-General. It was introduced to recognise Australian sporting achievements and the 18,015 recipients included former competitors, coaches, office holders, sports scientists and people who maintained sporting facilities and services.

With their baby due on Kieran's birthdate in March, Kerry had retired from bike racing. She appreciated her time on the tandem, but was looking forward to the change. She wrote in their annual Christmas letter:

> Kieran and I are two of the luckiest people due to the opportunities we have had and most of all because these experiences have brought us closer together. It's very nice to be home at last and beginning to live a life outside of cycling. At the same time, it's a challenge, because cycling has been integral to our relationship. We are both very excited about the baby and keen to start some renovating ideas on our house. We are really looking forward to going back to Port Lincoln and Thistle Island soon.

From now on, I was going to need male pilots.

The Australian Paralympic Committee found them by using the AIS (Australian Institute of Sport) database and matching Kieran with an eligible rider of suitable experience, similar body mass and matchable power outputs. Under UCI (Union Cycliste Internationale) rules, to apply to be a pilot for a para-cyclist, a professional cyclist must not participate in any UCI Tour for 24 months. Kieran's next pilot was Darren Harry, a sprinter from Western Australia. Darren was a training partner of another Australian sprint cycling champion, Darryn Hill, and had won the men's tandem sprint open gold at the Sydney Paralympics with Paul Clohessy.

Tandem riding needs teamwork and any pair needs to work together and for each other. I have observed countless examples of champion cyclists paired up for tandem racing who have not been able to get the bike moving effectively. So, it is important for me to get along with my pilots and I try hard to foster a close personal relationship. From a personality point of view, Darren and I were not the perfect mix. He was more forceful, dominant and aggressive; I am more reserved, relaxed and pliable. However, we combined well when it came to riding the tandem. On the track, Darren was ruthless. He seemed happy to bump and rough up our opponents. This does happen, especially in sprint racing, and we won lots of races together. I hoped that he would leave this on the track, but he was a little like this off the track as well. He is an intense character and I found it difficult to relax and unwind in his company. But I admired Darren as a cyclist. He was talented and strong. Somehow, we both managed to put aside our differences to make a successful tandem team. He was really the first male pilot that I had properly trained with, and I learnt a lot about cycling from him.

Australian team coach, Kevin McIntosh was also aware of the tension between the riders in his champion tandem team:

> I've never seen a more competitive athlete on the bike than Darren, and Kieran is one of the fairest cyclists I know. There were several aspects of the relationship that Kieran didn't like, but we found out about these after the Games. If we had known at the time, we would have dealt with them. But it is important to remember that it had a lot to do with success, because we had to win gold medals to be funded. In Sydney and in Athens we won nearly half the Australian gold medals and in Kieran and Darren we had the best combination for success. We had to manage this – sometimes we did it well and sometimes we didn't.

When I think of Darren, I can't help but smell coffee. He would always turn up at the track with a mug of plunger coffee, so strong that the spoon would almost stand up in the mug. Darren was adamant that I should try some. I managed to avoid his dreaded coffee, but eventually he wore me down and I drank a small cup.

It was vile and all I could taste for the whole day was this coffee. It hasn't put me off coffee altogether, but I like it weak now and the smell takes me back to those times.

In March 2002, the Track Nationals were held at the Dunc Gray velodrome in Sydney. Because there were less than three entries for the mixed tandem and the men's tandem, medals were awarded in relation to how close times were to the Australian records for their particular divisions. Kieran and Darren were the fastest qualifiers in the 200 m fly with 10.916, but came away with a silver medal because of the revised scoring system. They picked up bronze in the Kilo.

We flew to the 2002 IPC Para-cycling Track World Championships in Altenstadt and Augsburg in Germany. We were fascinated by our accommodation in army barracks used by a parachuting division (paratroopers), but not by the Augsburg track. It was only 200 m long (as compared to the normal 250 m) and this caused problems. The track felt like a big saucer. As you came out of one bend, you were straight into the next. It was so hazardous that they changed the sprint race to a 200 m fly. The officials felt it was too dangerous to have two tandems competing on the track simultaneously. Because of the extra g-force we rode on our strongest and heaviest frame and even then, we could feel the back disc (and our strongest wheel) start to flex under the strain. The tandem was leaving tyre marks around the bends as the bike skipped sideways. The g-forces tended to push the bike up towards the fence and when exiting the corners Darren did a brilliant job of holding the front of the bike down.

Darren and I won both the amended Sprint/200 m fly in 10.806 seconds and the Kilo in 1:05.46 minutes. Although Darren was primarily a sprinter, we had entered the road races as well.

We didn't go well in the time trial event and I wasn't keen to compete in the much longer road race around Altenstadt in the alpine foothills of Upper Bavaria because it had rained all night. The overall length of the road race was longer than usual and was made up of seven laps of a shorter tricky route. Each lap was difficult with tight corners and a nasty little hill – and the roads were just a sheet of water! It continued to rain and I didn't want to race. I tried to tell my coaches that it was just too dangerous, but Darren was keen and they dragged me out. We didn't warm up, but once the race started we got competitive. Darren is a risk taker and it turned out to be an advantage. It didn't help me, though, to pass numerous ambulances treating riders who had come off. Augsburg roads have many painted bike lanes and I often felt our wheels slipping on these. Under the circumstances, we finished a very creditable fourth, but it remains in my memory as one of the hardest events I've ever raced in. I found it frightening to lean the bike into the bends and felt tense throughout the race. When the fear is so intense, it is an inner battle to go harder. It was still raining when the medallists stood on the podium. We didn't hang around to watch!

I consider Darren to be the best of my pilots when it came to controlling the tandem. On a training run in Germany I remember coming down a mountain when a tyre blew out exiting a bend. I was looking around to see where I was likely to land, but Darren managed to keep the bike upright and we dismounted in normal fashion, skin intact. The Australian squad stopped to see how we were and we all wandered over to see where we would have finished up if Darren hadn't done such an expert job. Next to the kerb was a small guardrail before an almost vertical descent. Now we had to get back to our hostel 18 km away. Australian banknotes are made of polypropylene polymer (plastic) and so we used a $20 note to patch the hole. Somebody quipped that it was a very expensive tyre patch, but it got us home.

The trip to Germany was the first of many overseas journeys that I would make without Kerry. My emails home express my loneliness – and disappointment with the food:

> A month away is a very long time, especially when I'm used to having you with me. I am missing you so much. Some of the team have turned up slightly overweight and our coaches have put us all on strictly controlled meals. If I'm sitting near the thinner girls, I usually score their leftovers. I don't like the German breakfasts anyway. I would love some Weet-Bix instead of bread rolls and jam. I am always hungry and looking for food. Dessert would be nice!

For three years in a row the Australian para-cycling squad trained in Avezzano, Italy. Avezanno once lay on the shores of Lake Fucino, Italy's largest lake, which was drained in the late 19th century. After the land was reclaimed, the city grew and wide fields became available for cultivation. The city was destroyed in 1915 by possibly the worst earthquake in the history of Italy with 30,000 fatalities.

Kevin McIntosh remembers the town with affection:

> Avezzano was an outdoor track, a good environment to train and we were welcomed every year by the community. The mayor and the city council would greet us when we arrived. There was always an exchanging of flags and gifts to make it official that we were honoured guests of the town. When we went into town for an ice cream or coffee, it was often free. It was a comfortable environment and there were few complaints, although there were always athletes who made it harder for the other athletes, and for us as coaches and officials.

Needing time to myself, I enjoyed exploring this area, even without permission from the Australian team officials. The only time I could do this was on 'rest days'. The surrounding mountains are steep and beautiful, with pretty walking trails. I found rest days hard to handle, so at my first camp there, I decided to get up very early and (without telling anyone) take the tandem for a ride by myself. I found a mountain road that went almost straight up and decided that I needed to get to the top. For at least two hours I rode very slowly up the mountain road and after reaching the summit, it was time to descend. Realising that if either the bike or the rider was damaged in any way there would be big trouble, I took it very easy coming down. It was fun riding on the opposite side of the road to our Australian way and I was delighted that no one had missed the tandem or me when I got back to our hotel.

The following year I took hiking boots to walk the trails. On another rest day, and without telling anyone, I decided to climb a different mountain. It took hours to get to the base and I started climbing straight up. After four hours I had passed all vegetation and had come to an area of only shale and rock. About to give up, I saw another climber and followed him to the top, where we rang the bell on the summit. From the top we could see a severe storm approaching, so to get down quickly my new friend took me down the dangerous shale side, where we ran and slid our way to the bottom in about 20 minutes. It was exhilarating, and thankfully the friendly climber returned me to our hotel by car. Although very sore, I tried not to show it, and being a rest day, I thought my coach hadn't missed me. But the story got out when I showed the video that I took of my escapade to 'friends' and the masseurs noticed all my scratches and bruises and began asking questions!

Kieran's coach had *missed him:*

> There was a balance in getting Kieran to do what he needed to do, and stopping him from doing what he wanted to do. A good example is the way Kieran treated the recovery days. These are critical and after one recovery day in Italy I went to have a chat. It went like this:
>
> 'Kieran ... how was your day off yesterday? I didn't see you around. Did you spend most of it in bed?'
>
> (After a short pause.) 'Yeahhhhh.'
>
> 'Tell me more. I can't see you staying in bed all day. Did you go for a walk?'
>
> 'Yeahhhh.'
>
> 'Oh, where did you go? Did you walk into town?'
>
> 'Yeah.'
>
> 'Maybe further?'
>
> (Silence.)
>
> 'Kieran, I know where you went!'
>
> If ever you get to see the video, it is clear that Kieran didn't slide down the mountain ... more like rolled down it! On the video you see the legs going faster and faster ... and then it goes sky ... earth ... sky ... earth ... sky ... earth. So we had to have a little chat about the recovery process. But at the end of the day he always turned up and performed. Kerry was the complete opposite. She generally did what we asked her to do ... but she couldn't control Kieran either.

Darren Harry was an aggressive rider and in a race against the British at the 2003 European Para-cycling Championships in Terplice (the Czech Republic), Kieran thought that he went too far.

It was an outdoor track and we were racing close to the British. I was surprised when Darren rode up the track and put his knee into the British pilot's hamstring. I could see that the British pilot was shocked and they dropped back. However, coming into the last lap and when Darren went to accelerate, his left foot pulled out of the pedal. Undeterred he continued to ride with only one foot and the bike was twitching all over the place. The British team came up alongside us as we went over the finish line. It was so close that it took a lap to find out that we had won by a tyre width. Darren was certainly a very determined sportsman. We had won again, but I felt we didn't need to be so aggressive.

The outdoor velodrome in Terplice was unusual because each lap was 333 m long. Having just won the 200 m sprints, we were confident that we could win the Kilo. We were the current world champions from the previous world titles and as such would race last and know what time we had to beat. There is a five-second countdown and from a standing start the clock is started. On a 106" gear we punched out from the blocks only to get 30 m and hear unusual noises coming from the bike. The force we had applied through the pedals at the start had bent the back end of the frame several degrees, kinking the chain stay tube. Our mechanics shook their heads in disbelief. We were granted a re-race, but on a borrowed bike and wary about breaking it too, we had lost some confidence and were far too tentative. We finished a disappointing tenth.

Mechanical issues were to affect our road race as well. The frame was flexing and twisting under pressure and the connecting chain between front and rear rider came off. We came twelfth.

After these championships, I took a break from tandem racing and Darren found another visually impaired cyclist to work with, a stoker (rear rider) called Leon Larkins.

While Kieran was away from para-cycling, Paralympic sport was getting a huge organisational and financial boost. In April 2003 the

Para-Cycling High-Performance Program was introduced. This program was funded by the Australian Sports Commission with the aim of providing the best possible training and competition opportunities for identified athletes. The aim was to deliver medal-winning performances at the Paralympic Games and World Championships. Para-athletes selected in this 'camp-based' program could train at their own State Academy of Sport, which in Kieran's case was the South Australian Sports Institute (SASI). On returning to cycling, he successfully applied to be a scholarship holder in this High-Performance Program.

It was time for me to prepare for Athens and the Australian Paralympic Committee gave me a choice of pilot. There were three potential candidates flown to Adelaide to meet and ride with me. I chose Tyson Lawrence. With my previous pilots, except Kerry of course, I only saw them maybe four times a year, so I trained a lot of the time on single bikes. Tyson came from Western Australia, which made it difficult to get together with him. I find my most effective training is on the tandem bike. In 2003 I was lucky to find a local training partner for the tandem, Mike Hoile. Now I could practice on the tandem in between visits from my assigned pilots. And Mike has remained one of my best friends.

One of the first reactions of people on entering a velodrome is amazement at the steepness of the banks at either end. Velodrome tracks are generally sloped from around 12 degrees on the relatively flat straights up to 47° at the steepest part of the banked turns (the shorter the track, the steeper the banking). It is extremely difficult to walk up a 47° incline – and very easy to slide down it!

Tyson Lawrence had broken his leg on a training ride (without me), so I was matched up with New South Welshman David Short.

At the National Championships, we were destined to meet the Harry–Larkins combination in the final. I was dreading coming up against Darren, my former pilot, and was expecting a tough and rough race.

Darren Harry was aware of the perils of a 42° incline and I remember how cleverly he chose that point. The race was just as I feared. Darren cut in front, slowed us up and forced us on to the fence at the top of the track. We hit our pedals on the wooden panelling and it was amazing that we didn't come off and slide down the track. But hitting the fence slowed us enough to get clear of them. Darren tried to keep covering us, but we dived down the track behind him to sprint away and win. Darren was later fined for dangerous riding tactics.

I had escaped and won another national competition, but the Australian Paralympic Committee had a few tricks up their sleeves.

Uncle Andy: *You've shown your romantic side now, Kieran. Perhaps we could spice this book up with a little more about your love life.*

Kieran: I was just so blessed that Kerry persevered with me. Riding tandems brings you physically into very close proximity with another person. It's probably fair to say that riding with Kerry was far more enjoyable than riding with my male tandem partners. Perhaps you'll have to leave the Mills and Boon stuff for your next book, Uncle Andy.

I've read and reread and written and rewritten your time with Darren Harry. Do you think we have been a little severe?

Perhaps, but I trust Darren will understand that this is all written from my perspective. After a very short stint with Eddie Hollands in Augsburg, Darren was my first male pilot. Any problems in our relationship socially were no doubt exacerbated by me. I really missed Kerry both as a rider and a travelling companion. Darren was a big step into the reality of tough tandem racing. I will always have huge respect for Darren and am thankful for all that he taught me.

The story of Kerry and you in Atlanta and of course the marriage proposal on Vancouver Island is a scenario just waiting for a movie script writer. Would you have retired had Sydney gone better for you both?

That's a good question. Maybe ... but I always get that itch to train again and return to the track. Somehow things never go as planned. One day I am going to have a perfect preparation and get the perfect result without any problems.

Well, Kieran, that's not about to happen anytime soon ...

7
Athens and politics

2004–2007

Only four months before the Athens Paralympics, 1992 Barcelona Olympian Robert Crowe was asked by the Australian Paralympic Committee to be Kieran's new pilot. Rob was already well into cycling retirement and by his own reckoning 10 kg overweight. At the Barcelona Olympics (12 years earlier) he and his teammates had been favourites for the road team time-trial gold medal, but Rob had punctured a tyre and this bad luck had caused the team to lose. Rob now had the chance to experience success and he took it enthusiastically. Along with the pain and suffering of this new training regime, he had to learn how to ride a tandem – and with an experienced partner. Their first serious time check was still five seconds off the qualifying time needed and ten seconds from any chance of a medal. Fortunately, they were given permission to delay their qualifying time until closer to the Games.

Time was spent looking at the bike and the gearing, and trying to match up their different styles. Kieran is a typical high cadence track rider. In cycling, cadence is the number of revolutions of the crank per minute, or the rate at which a cyclist is pedalling. Rob was better suited to the road, with low cadence and bigger gears. To bring the two styles closer together, trainers sent Kieran into the Adelaide Hills pushing big gears and towing a cart filled with bricks. Rob fitted brakes and a spinning gear to a track bike and then tried to keep up with fast-moving groups of riders on the road. It worked and the pair qualified just two weeks before the Games, but they were still way off the Paralympic record, which Kieran so badly wanted to break.

Interestingly it was noticed that we lost our line going into corners. A myotherapist (a specialist in musculoskeletal treatment) worked on Rob's upper back and neck muscles, helping Rob keep his head higher so that he could better line up the approach to corners and save centimetres.

The Australian Paralympic Committee had more surprises in store. They had organised *two* pilots for me: Robert Crowe for the pursuit, road race and road time trial and David Short for the Kilo, track time trial and the sprints. There was nothing in the UCI rules to say that you could not do this. I had to adjust for each rider. Not only were their styles very different, but I had to dramatically alter the position of my back when riding. Rob was tall and so I could raise my back up. David was short, requiring me to flatten down in an attempt to tuck in behind David's smaller body frame. Rob would fly from Victoria to train with me in Adelaide and I would fly to Sydney to train with David.

The whole Australian Paralympic cycling team was in for a shock. Australia had been granted a mere ten cycling places for the Athens Games and National Paralympic Program coach Kevin McIntosh was angry. He told reporters:

> This news is devastating for the Australian cycling team, ranked number one in the world. In fact, we have held that rank for the last four years. The United States team have only managed to get into the top three over that same period and they have been granted 15 cycling places in Athens. At our current National Championships, we have broken eight world records with two days of competition left to go. Unless we get

> a better share of places, we will be leaving gold medal winners at home. This allocation is political – and we are going to fight it all the way to the top if we have to!

Team manager, Elsa Lepore, said that Australia had believed the number of spots handed out would be performance based:

> Given that we were ranked number one at the Sydney Paralympics where we had a team of 15, and that we have maintained that rank since, we should get the maximum number of spots. The International Paralympics Committee have used a ranking system that we do not consider was interpreted in a logical way. They allowed some nations to accrue points from regional competitions, which was contrary to what we believed the interpretation should be. It's criminal and it's going to cost a lot of money to fight it.

The Australian Paralympic movement, with the full support of Cycling Australia, appealed to the IPC's Executive Committee. This proved unsuccessful, so the two Australian sporting bodies appealed to the International Court of Arbitration, at an estimated cost of around $50,000. Again, they were refused any extra cycling spots.

A nasty situation arose. To make the Paralympics team, a candidate needs qualifying points, and these are accumulated from precisely recorded times. Gold medal potential is always important to selection as well. An athlete with a better chance at medalling will get priority, but getting these qualifying points is very important, as Kieran was about to find out. The problems with selection arose because the rules used to select the Australian team were not updated to cover one para-cyclist having two pilots.

This left a loophole, which other para-cyclists used to gain selection and, in the process, push me out of the team. I now had one set of qualifying points with Robert Crowe and another set of points with David Short. When both were combined, I gained selection comfortably. The other teams that coveted a place in the squad argued that the selection criteria documentation only referred to using one set of points and by separating my points another team outscored me. There were ten spots in the Australian team going to Athens. My tandem team ranking moved from seventh to 11th position after I was classified as two separate teams and only because I had been given different pilots. Two teams could challenge for my place in the squad: Darren Harry and Leon Larkins, and then Jenny Macpherson and Lyn Lepore. Disappointingly it ended up in court.

During this uncertainty, I continued training with both pilots. David had accessed a lawyer who gave us good advice pro bono.

The appeal process is two tiered, with the appeal being first heard by the APC's Appeal Tribunal with any subsequent appeal to be heard by the Court of Arbitration for Sport. The selection battle went from one court to another. When it went to a Court of Law and the content of the selection document was prioritised, they were out. When it went to the Court of Arbitration for Sport and was judged from a more sporting perspective, they were back in the Australian team. Journalist Stan Gordon reported in the Port Lincoln Times *in September 2004 the response of their lawyer, Greg Walsh:*

> They were devastated and none the wiser as to how such a situation had arisen. Kieran, who is legally blind, had to get his wife to read the letter to him which, even to someone well versed in the rules, was difficult to follow. The appeal is obviously an extremely significant one, as it raises fundamental issues in respect of procedural fairness and natural justice. His non-selection is a travesty in itself and the appeal will examine

> the conduct and role of the Australian Paralympic Committee. Fundamentally, he should be on the team.

When the team left Australia for a pre-Games training camp in Italy, I was technically in the squad and although quietly confident that I would be competing for Australia, the issue was still before the courts.

Arriving at the training camp in Avezanno, Italy, I was disappointed that there was still tension between those involved in the legal battle for Australian selection. It didn't help that my place in the team was being challenged by fellow cyclist Lyn Lepore, whose husband was the team mechanic and sister, Elsa, the team manager.

To make matters worse, coach Kevin McIntosh was forced to return to Australia. In the space of 14 days he lost his mother, father-in-law and sister-in-law. He was away from the team for a week and in that time the tension grew. This was all too apparent to Kevin when he returned to Avezanno:

> Elsa Lepore was team manager in Athens and there was conflict there between her and Kieran. Kieran wasn't sure where Elsa's allegiance would lie, but Elsa was straight down the line in that situation. She was there for the team and no one else. She treated Kieran and Lyn equally. However, I wasn't there for seven days and I came back to a divided team. There were two parties and I took them to the mountain and we discussed the problem. There were tears and we walked away from the top of the mountain as one team.

Only eight days before the opening ceremony, officials informed Kieran, David and Rob that they had missed out on selection. The Court of Arbitration in Sport had ruled that fellow Australian Lyn Lepore deserved her place in the team.

I knew that this decision had nothing to do with the officials and Australian team support in Italy. The Australian coaches were still prepared to work with us, and allowed us to stay with the team in their training camp accommodation. I wanted to stay with the team, but David felt awkward and uncomfortable with this position. So, we respected his feelings and moved into a nearby hotel.

Kevin McIntosh was sad to see them go:

> The thing I was most disappointed about was that Kieran, David and Robert left the team. I should never have let that happen. I asked them not to go, but they voted amongst themselves and left. I let them down.

The legal battles over selection continued back in Australia. Over the three-month period, five court cases were heard. Their story now had become controversial and newsworthy and so they had a film crew following them around making a documentary. This television crew turned out to be very supportive and encouraging and helped maintain positivity.

Four days after the Australian Paralympic team moved from Italy to Athens for the Games, we followed them. Now we had to get to Greece 'under our own steam', paying our own way and dragging our bikes and bags up and down escalators, on to crowded trains and through narrow doors. Nobody in Australia knew where we were and it's probably fair to say that we weren't all that sure either!

We were still determined to race for Australia and continued to train at every opportunity. We had heard of two other means of entry into the competition.

For those athletes from developing countries who had not made the qualification criteria, there were wildcard entries. This hardly applied to

Kieran and his pilots and our homeland Australia, but there were other possibilities for filling some remaining spots.

A bipartite commission invitation allocation gave 15 athletes entry if they applied in writing and had international sport class status. This was set up to ensure there was a good spread of athletes in all the events, to encourage participation from all parts of the globe and, most importantly for Kieran, to ensure that all potential medallists got to take part.

Another means of entry was left to the International Paralympic Committee. They had the right to allocate qualification slots to athletes. If there were spots not allocated or reallocated by the established deadlines and spots left unused, they could be redistributed at the discretion of the IPC.

So there was still a chance, but time was running out!

We booked into a hotel as close to the Paralympic Village as possible. Unable to train at the velodrome, we rode around Athens trying to stay tuned and ready to race if the call came through. For the rest of that four-day period we sat in our hotel rooms and waited. It was like being in the middle of a cyclone. Everything was whizzing around us. People were telling us this and that. Officials were working behind the scenes to get us into the team. The courts were handing out verdicts. Everyone seemed to have an opinion. All we could do was try to relax, stay positive and concentrate on being as ready as possible, just in case.

Greg Hartung and the Australian Paralympic Committee were doing everything they could. They applied to the International Paralympic Committee for an additional team member. While the Committee accepted the bona fides of the CAS (Court of Arbitration in Sport) finding, Australian chef de mission Paul Bird said that the APC believed

Kieran had a genuine argument to also compete on his competitive merits. After deliberation, the IPC announced on Thursday night that it had granted the Australian team a 144th spot – an extra position – to accommodate Kieran. A delighted Paul Bird congratulated the IPC for agreeing to consider their application and seeing the logic of their case – and quickly phoned Kieran with the good news.

Five hours before the Opening Ceremony, word came through that we had a qualification slot. We didn't have time to celebrate. I messaged Kerry at home with our children: 'We are in, baby! We are in! We are in!' We quickly packed up, left the hotel, got accredited at the Games venue and then went straight to the track. We had one practice and then left to settle into the Village. Our pursuit was on the following day! We were well-received by the Australian team, who had been following our fortunes. Not much was said because everyone was focused on their own preparation and event and it is always most important to keep the atmosphere in the Village positive and supportive.

Kevin McIntosh was thrilled with the news and there were tears when the four reunited, but even he was unaware of the perseverance and sheer doggedness of the lawyers and officials who had created this chance:

> Modra should always have been the first selected into the games. Because of Tyson breaking a leg and then Kieran's times with David weren't great and then with Robert even worse, this left them on the cusp of selection. We always regarded Kieran and Robert as gold medallists and Kieran and David medallists. David put more into the bike as it went on and got better. But I wasn't aware of the whole process and how they got in, and only found out at the Opening Ceremony.

Members of Kieran's family had travelled to Greece to watch him race. Theo (Kieran's father) remembers the uncertainty:

> Our daughter Tania and her husband Simon were living and working in Belgium. We spent some time in Rome and then had planned to meet up with them in Athens. We had all bought tickets to watch Kieran, Rob and David cycle at the Paralympics and then waited anxiously while the courts decided whether they could participate. Communication wasn't as clever as it is today and so for long periods of time we just didn't know what was happening. The last we heard was that they were out, but we had the tickets and decided to turn up at the venue. Tania was scanning the competitors warming up. Suddenly she said, 'I think I can see Kieran's back!' We knew that they only allowed competitors in that area, so we all got very excited!

Not only did Rob and I have a short preparation and little practice on the track, we were up against Dutch world champions, Jan Mulder and Pascal Schoots.

Both riders were former European professionals, until Mulder succumbed to a congenital eye disease. Jan Mulder had a formidable reputation. He had dominated the pursuit event and both Kieran and Rob were well aware of his record and talent.

In the pursuit, competitors start on opposite sides of the track and attempt to catch their opponents. The four teams with the best times from the opening round progress to the medal round, where the first fastest races the second fastest for gold and silver, and third races fourth for bronze. If a competitor catches and passes the opponent, they win the race, although they may choose to continue, usually to try to set a record.

In our first round of the pursuit, my dream became a reality when we clocked 4:21 minutes, a new Paralympic record. However, Mulder and Schoots were progressing through as well to an inevitable showdown. The final was a defining race in my cycling career. I had developed great respect for Jan Mulder. We wanted gold so badly. We just went flat out and kept gaining on the Dutch champions. I felt ecstatic when we lapped them, meaning that the gold medal was ours. But we kept pushing and clocked 4:23. It was the first gold medal for Australia at Athens, thanks to so many people who worked so hard for us behind the scenes. Rob was euphoric. He could finally put to bed his disappointment at Barcelona. But in Athens I had two pilots, with David Short as my sprinter. I didn't want to win gold with just one of them.

After this race, Jan Mulder announced his retirement from international cycling, ending a long and distinguished career. It also concluded his reign as the para-tandem pursuit champion. To be caught and lapped is an embarrassment and humiliation to any pursuit rider. A new kid was on the block!

I paid due respect to Jan after the race. I made a point of speaking to him. I wanted to congratulate him and tell him that in many ways he was my idol. I had heard a lot about him and I aspired to try to get to his level and race with him.

On the following day, David and I rode a disappointing race in the Kilo with a seventh placing, but we still had the sprints to go. We began to have equipment problems. We heard a clicking noise coming from a wheel. They glue the tyres on to the rims and we thought it might have been an air bubble. So, we changed the wheel. We started the sprint and after half a lap there was a huge bang as our new tyre blew out. The front wheel slipped sideways and so did we. We were only going slowly so there was little damage to the bike ... and to us. We expected a restart and had to convince the officials that the bang was our tyre and not a disqualification pistol! Of course, now the only spare we had was the clicky wheel and so on it went.

We got the restart and won and so proceeded on to our next opponents, a team from Japan. We won the first heat and then made a big mistake. The clicky tyre had survived the last race and we should have changed it. When you race tandems, you listen acutely to what noises the bike is making. You can hear when things begin to go wrong. I was aware that strange noises were coming from the front. On the last bend and only 80 m from the finish, and when we were going flat out for the line at a speed of 65 kph, the clicky front tyre of the tandem rolled off the front rim. For some distance the bike was still upright running on a wheel without a tyre. The carbon front wheel was breaking up and bits of it were flying everywhere. I couldn't see what was happening, but the bike was twitching all over the place. I knew we were going to go down and when we did we slid 25 m along the bare wooden track. We both received burn marks from the wood and lots of splinters. Most of the falls I have happen so fast, but this one seemed to take forever. I so wanted off that bike!

David showed great skill and quick thinking during that accident. He held the bike upright for about 20 m, and might have kept it that way if he wasn't watching the front wheel shrink. He made a conscious decision to drop the bike down the track, so that we slid towards the pit area. If he had dropped it pointing up-track, we would have hit the track hard. If he had continued much further the front wheel would have collapsed, the front forks dug into the track and we would have both been catapulted over our handlebars.

The Japanese rode past the carnage to win that heat, and I was stretchered off the track to join David in the medical room for further examination. The officials arrived there soon after and asked us if we wanted to continue. We looked more like wounded soldiers, but with a new front wheel and tyre we beat the Japanese team 2–1. We had only 45 minutes to prepare for the chance to win gold. We were a mess! We had skin torn off our arms, legs and shoulders. It probably only made us more determined, because our job wasn't finished. We were a team. It was David's chance to win and I was riding for him. I was so focused on the bike, I was just numb basically. All the pain was put right out of mind.

In the gold medal race-off against Slovakia David and I lost the first heat and had bike trouble again. We were both sore and believed the pursuit for gold was dashed; surely there was no way we could match a fresher team and win. So we talked over the situation with our coach and changed our strategy. The Slovakians were faster than us, so we started to look at our own strengths rather than worrying about theirs. We focused on what we do well and decided the best tactic was to keep our speed high and prevent our opponents from accelerating past.

It was a brutal test of strength and will, but it worked. We won the next two heats to claim the ultimate prize – and David got to mount the podium just like Rob. I couldn't imagine winning with one and not the other. Our trio was complete.

In Athens, the administrators combined the road time trial and the road race for only one set of medals. Kieran and Rob won the time trial and usually this was rewarded with a gold medal. However, while leading the 110 km road race, they crashed badly again (for the third time at these Games) at the turnaround point and damaged their back wheel. Officials later apologised to them for the condition of that turnaround point. A bollard placed there was faulty and had leaked water across the track. Inevitably the damaged wheel came loose and with a slow wheel change, they fell back in the field to finish eighth. When the results of their two races were combined, the result was bronze.

Kieran had made history – the first rider to compete in all five track events and now he was taking home two gold, one bronze and a world record. And without some considerable help from officialdom and a good dose of self-belief, he could easily have missed the Games altogether. In an ironic postscript, the team that took them to court to gain selection were the only members of the Australian para-cycling team to miss out on winning a medal. They were to do better in future years.

David Short is understandably a great admirer of Kieran:

> In the beginning it looked like all the training was for nothing. We all worked to keep our spirits up. And then we had three very nasty crashes, the second of which was gruesome. Rob and I shared the load, but Kieran endured an enormous workload under extreme pressure. It was a challenge, but we all got there. It's a credit to the athlete Kieran is. He is an amazing man.

Asked by journalists what had caused the most disruption, the five appeals or the falls, David replied:

> Tough one, both equal on the day, but the original appeal battle would have been the toughest. The three of us have become very tight. Each one has been down at different times and now we are very close. When Rob and I sent Kieran to the masseurs and medical staff we would jokingly say, 'Please rebuild him.' Thank goodness that it was a bike race, because he can hardly walk now. It's been an amazing battle to get here and probably one of the hardest day's racing – just fantastic!

Sydney lawyer Greg Walsh, who had acted on behalf of Kieran throughout the weeks of court cases, was quick to congratulate Kieran and Rob after the pursuit, and told Stan Grant of the Port Lincoln Times*:*

> The winning of the gold medal by Kieran Modra completely vindicates Cycling Australia's selection of him on four separate occasions for Athens. But for the intervention of the IPC a grave injustice would have occurred. We are all proud that Kieran had an opportunity to win Australia a gold medal.

After the Athens success, Kieran was named the Australian Male Paralympian of the Year.

I felt honoured but with reservations. It's a token of respect for what we've gone through and a nice acknowledgement. But the best thing about the awards night was that I could acknowledge my co-riders, because out of all the people that supported me on the roller coaster road to the Paralympics, most of all it was them. I am very proud of them. The downside of these award nights is that they compare athletes, but everyone there has achieved. It's nice to be presented with awards, but I think about the people who didn't win – it doesn't mean they've achieved less than I have.

Following a Paralympic Games, I generally take a year off from tandem cycling and during that time my pilot usually finds another pathway in life or another para-athlete to ride with. After every Paralympics I have wanted to retire. This level of competition is stressful and hard work. But after a long break I get the bug back. The administrators help this along by suggesting riders I could work with, events I might win, and countries that are holding the World or European Championships. They know I like to travel and they cleverly mention all the venues around the world and the nearby tourist attractions!

Rob Crowe had retired again to start a new business and David Short was now heavily involved in coaching other cyclists. Fortunately, Tyson Lawrence's leg had healed and we renewed our partnership.

The Arafura Games is one of the few events where able-bodied athletes compete in the same events as disabled. We attended the Arafura Games in Darwin in May 2007, but weren't popular with all on race day. Our team manager entered us into the road race to broaden our experience, but the Darwin race administrators hadn't informed other competitors that they would be sharing the road with tandems. We came second. We were happy, but the locals weren't and there were complaints. I had talked my good mate, Mike Hoile, into entering his own tandem into the race as well. We managed to organise a stoker for Mike, but he was very inexperienced. When Mike started to power up, the stoker couldn't keep his legs moving quickly enough. The stoker's torso started to wobble, the bike wobbled and although they were quite dangerous to be near, they were fun to watch.

Over the next few years Kieran and Tyson went on a record-breaking spree.

In Bordeaux, France at the 2007 World Track and Road Championships we broke our own pursuit world record creating the new benchmark time of 4:20.891. We also won bronze medals in the sprints, the Kilo and the road time trials. Although pleased with another world record and gold medal, I felt responsible for overdoing things. I love to explore and the area around Bordeaux had so much to see. I organised our training runs to take in as many of the local sights as possible. I had heard of the Dune of Pilat (Dune du Pilat) the largest in Europe at 2.7 km long, 500 m wide and 110 m high. On the day before racing for medals we set off to visit this spectacular dune, 60 km north on the French coast. It was worth seeing, but we lost our way a few times and by the time we got back to Bordeaux, we had ridden 160 km. This is too far to ride on the day before the trials for championship events began and we both felt tired. Our coaches didn't find out, but maybe we could have done even better at those championships with more sensible preparation.

We were the world para-pursuit champions and things were looking good for Beijing ... too good.

8 Beijing and the bad boy

2008–2011

Kieran had built up a good relationship with the experienced head coach Kevin McIntosh, who had moved from being the Victorian junior coach to becoming head coach at the Western Australian Institute of Sport. In 1999 he became the national para-cycling head coach for Cycling Australia. In early 2005 he was appointed head coach of the Australian Paralympic Cycling program. Only eight months out from the Beijing Games he was sacked from this position and subsequently took a cycling coaching position with the South Australian Sports Institute. He was replaced by James Victor, the son of Mike Victor, who was the President of Cycling Australia from 2000 until 2009.

Kevin was devastated:

> It destroyed me. I got up in the morning because I was coaching the Paralympic team, and to have that taken away from me was not only a large injustice, but a huge disappointment. I had recently lost my son and I was struggling; I asked for help, but didn't get it – and the powers that be thought I couldn't cope. In fact, they took support away. I started out with a full-time and two part-time assistant coaches, and ended up with one part-time assistant. Kieran didn't know any of this. I was manoeuvred out, and so close to the Games, but that's life and we've all moved on.

I missed Kevin. He trusted me to be able to monitor myself and prepare effectively for competition. I had proved time after time that I could peak for the Paralympic Games and other championships, not only with gold medals but often with world records as well.

I believed Kevin was doing a brilliant job. He was passionate about his work and many para-athletes blossomed under his enthusiasm and encouragement. Training athletes with disabilities is a special task. Each disability is different. Each athlete is different. It is important to get to know these athletes and train them appropriately, mindful of their limitations. Kevin understood this principle, listened to the athletes and set up individualised training programs with skill and a good measure of sensitivity.

On a lighter note, Kevin was also getting me to wear shoes. It was a habit that I found difficult to acquire. As a young lad, I was so used to running around on the farm in bare feet. We would come home from school and throw off our shoes and socks and only put them back on for school the next day. This habit stayed with me and because it's difficult to walk in bicycle shoes, I would remove them and walk everywhere barefooted.

In cycling the feet are particularly important, because all of the cyclist's power and pressure goes through them. The coaches were concerned that without the protection provided by shoes, Kieran was almost certain to damage his feet. Over time, Kevin managed to get him to understand this:

> When we were training in Avezzano, Italy, and staying in hotels, to walk around without shoes showed contempt for their culture and hospitality – and we had to protect feet from injury and infection. The athletes are there to compete. That's always the priority. I had numerous discussions with Kieran. In the end the compromise was that he would wear shoes in the

lobby and could go bare-footed in his room. These days Kieran is more responsible with his footwear.

To add some weight to Kieran's respect for his old coach, in 2000, 2002 and 2004 Kevin McIntosh was named Australian Paralympic Committee Coach of the Year. He was named Cycling Australia's Coach of the Year in 2000 and inducted into the International Paralympic Committee Hall of Fame in 2008.

I felt the timing for a change of coaches was poor. James had brought in his own support team as well, so there were suddenly a lot of new faces around doing things differently. I began to write letters to management about this situation. Because I was one of the older athletes in the squad and had already been to four Paralympic Games, many of the unhappy athletes would come to me with complaints, which I would pass on. I had nothing to lose. My unhappy colleagues had more to lose and wanted to remain anonymous. They were happy for me to voice their disapproval, but did not support me when things came to a head.

Despite these tensions, the new coach stayed and the team was farewelled at Sydney Airport by Thérèse Rein, wife of then Prime Minister Kevin Rudd. The team flew to China on a chartered Qantas jet, a luxury previously reserved for Olympians only.

We settled into our Village and I focused on my training. All the disputes were handled mostly by small group discussions. Rumours abounded and this did nothing to unite the team.

Although there was not the team harmony of previous Games, the Australian team in Beijing performed well in their respective events. Nick Dean was again the assistant chef de mission in charge of the cyclists. He was experienced in this role, having already worked with many Paralympic winter and summer teams. Nick considers that team tension is not unusual:

> There are always tensions in any group and there are teams within teams, particularly with the elite, because they generally can't achieve unless they are like that. Effective team management understands that and responds quickly, clearly and fairly. There was disharmony in the cycling team. They often tend to relate to one coach and if that coach isn't the team coach, there is often an issue. It is unusual to have harmony! It is a dynamic environment. When they talk about the Australian team, they are talking about a group that only comes together every four years for about three weeks. Within this group are teams within teams within teams. A basketball team needs harmony because basketball is a team sport and relies on teamwork. A cycling team, however, is made up of individuals and pairs (for the tandem), each focused on their own event. Each sub-group sticks together, but the public are led to believe that all the Australians are all relating actively and effectively with each other as a single cohesive unit. Before each of the Games there are often athletes fighting for positions through the courts.

Opening ceremonies usually involve a lot of standing around and waiting in team groups to enter the arena. Having entered and walked to the area designated for the Australian team, the athletes must then wait for all other teams to do likewise. It makes for a long day and can go late into the evening.

In Beijing, all athletes who were to compete on the day following the Opening Ceremony were told very clearly that they were not to attend the Opening Ceremony. Tyson and I were in this group. But I had other ideas. The Opening Ceremony is a highlight and I don't like missing out. I was determined to go and because I had lost respect for the coach and authority, I felt that it didn't matter if I estranged myself further by breaking the rules.

Dressed in the Australian Paralympic uniform, I set off for the ceremony. But Australian team officials were waiting and challenged me at the exit door of the Village. The conversation went something like this:

'Where are you going?'

'I'm going to the Opening Ceremony.'

'No you're not!'

'Yes I am!'

'No you're not!'

'Yes I am!'

'No you're not!'

'Yes I am!'

And with that, I exited the Village and headed for the bus specially designated for the Australian team to take us to the Niaochao National Stadium, the main arena for the 2008 Beijing Games and better known to the world as 'the bird's nest'. The Australian bus had already left and probably just as well for me. There was a good chance that the Australian officials on board that bus would again have tried to exclude me. So I jumped on the next bus going, one of many transporting the Chinese team. I felt a little conspicuous surrounded by the Chinese home team, but it got me to the venue.

Assistant chef de mission, Nick Dean saw Kieran there:

> He was a naughty boy – but it was nothing more than that. He wasn't wicked, he didn't break the law, he didn't abscond, or go out of the town, or shimmy up a flagpole and steal a

> flag. Cycling Australia was team management there and they made it clear to Kieran that he wasn't to march at the Opening Ceremony. Kieran was just as determined to go and as we waited for a long time in a group just outside the main stadium for the call up, Kieran hid. It is important to remember that Kieran wasn't the only athlete who needed close management. There were many others. It's the same with the able-bodied athletes as well – they can be a handful to manage.

At the Opening Ceremony, an Australian official told me to be back at the athletes' Village by 11 pm or else. When I did return, I was immediately hauled before Australia's chef de mission, Darren Peters. I am not sure how close I came to being sent home, but in my dressing-down it was made quite clear that there was an expectation of a gold medal on the following day.

On the following morning, we felt this added pressure to perform. Our confidence grew when we broke our own world record, set the previous year in France in a preliminary round of the individual pursuit with a time of 4:18.961. We worked our way through to the final. Tyson and I were nervous, but feeling really good before the gold medal race. In the preliminary heats, we would often catch up to our more inexperienced rivals and that ended the race. Sometimes the officials stopped timing the race when this happened. I asked the timers to keep their instruments running, because no matter what happened, we wanted to have another crack at our world record.

My words to the officials were prophetic. To our surprise, we caught and passed the Spaniards Christian Venge and David Llaurado. The gold medal was won, but to cap off a remarkable day we broke the world record again in a time of 4:18.166.

As we cycled around the track after the race, with me proudly flying the Australian flag above my head, Tyson noticed familiar faces in the crowd. We stopped to acknowledge our parents who had come down to the rails to greet us. And we were delighted to stop again to high five an old favourite.

Kevin McIntosh had come to the velodrome as a spectator to enjoy the pair's success:

> I was in Beijing to be inducted into the Paralympic Hall of Fame, but had planned to go to the velodrome anyway. I had such a good relationship with Kieran and had coached Tyson for a long time in Western Australia. There was no way that I was going to miss their races!

The next day we followed this up with a bronze in the 1 km time trial. In the road races, we were not as successful, with a fifth in the tandem road time trial and an 11th in the road race.

No doubt all medals are valued by athletes, but the Beijing medals are exquisite with inlaid jade in three colours. They are my favourites and I am only disappointed that I didn't get a silver medal so that I could have the complete set. It was common knowledge around the Village that some of the gold in the medals was almost certainly mined in Australia – so it was coming back home!

I enjoyed Beijing and because we had entered only four events, there was more time to enjoy the Paralympic experience. I like to eat so I especially enjoyed the food halls, which were about 200 m long, and there were so many choices. We were supposed to ride only around the Village, a 6 km circuit, but we soon got bored with this.

We wanted to ride around Beijing. The biggest fear was the traffic, but the Chinese had reduced vehicle traffic in Beijing for the Olympics to minimise smog. So we ventured out and found that it was quite safe to ride the streets. Furthermore, the Chinese people embraced us. Whenever we stopped we were swamped with people asking for autographs or taking photos and 'selfies'. Being the stoker and hands-free, I could take photos and movies while riding. I taped my movie camera to my helmet (unusual then but now an easily acquired accessory) and now have wonderful videotapes of these adventures around the Beijing streets and through Tiananmen Square.

As had happened many times before, a new pilot was waiting for me to return to Australia to begin preparations for the London Paralympics.

Scott McPhee was the youngest and lightest of Kieran's pilots. Despite being only 19 years of age, Scott had more than ten years of experience in racing, and he was South Australian, making it easier to train with Kieran. He was also going to be a support in other ways. Scott's career was at a junction. He had finished juniors and was deciding whether to race in Europe or join a domestic team. National coach, Tim Decker, suggested Scott aim for the Paralympics. Once committed to tandem racing and paired with Kieran, Scott put his law degree at the University of Adelaide on hold.

I appreciated Scott's dedication. He is a very talented cyclist and adapted to tandems easily. Because I am not allowed to drive, Scott would leave his Wayville home every day and travel roughly 20 km out of his way to pick me up in Hallett Cove and take me to my work at the School for Vision Impaired. After my work finished he would collect me and we would head to the South Australian Sports Institute for a two-hour gym session. Scott would always drop me back home, sometimes as late as 10 pm. On Tuesdays we would ride together, beginning with a 60 km recovery ride and followed by an intensive three-hour track session, often chasing a motorbike around the track. I was back at work on Wednesdays and the training load was lighter – a 30-minute ergo session for me and later an hour in the gym followed by a massage. On Thursdays, a two-hour gym session was followed by another three hours of intensive track work. I worked again at the school on Fridays, our rest day. The weekend was not for resting; Saturdays were tough. Three hours of intensive work on the track was followed by two hours of ergo sprints and all at maximum effort. Sundays were easy. We rode 100 km as recovery! Not all weeks were like this. Our training program worked in cycles, allowing our bodies to recover before starting the next challenging sequence.

As independent as I am with public transport, Scott was willing to travel to ensure my safety. Often we would meet up and drive to training venues, because public transport to those places was difficult and time consuming. I was especially thankful and appreciative after late-night sessions, when buses only run hourly. From my home to the Superdrome by public transport on a good day takes two hours each way, and longer at night and on weekends, so Scott's help was invaluable.

To get to London, Kieran and Scott needed to spend around 24 hours together most weeks, often seeing more of each other than their families. They also spent much of 2011 travelling around the globe. The schedule began in Australia where they had immediate success, winning the road race and coming second in the time trial at the National Championships. They won gold in the road race at the Oceania Championships in Caloundra, Queensland, and silver in the same event at the 2011 UCI Para-cycling Road World Cup in Sydney.

Their international itinerary was tight. On 28 and 29 May they were racing in Italy; from 2 to 5 June in Belgium, and from 10 to 12 June in Spain.

At the 2011 UCI Para-cycling Track World Championships in Montichiari, Italy, the pair came first in the 4 km tandem pursuit and broke the world record again in the process, setting a new time of 4:17.780.

We competed in the Tour of Belgium, an annual five-day series of road races held in late May. The first Ronde van België or Tour de Belgique was raced in 1908. It was gruelling having to race every day, often once in the morning and again in the afternoon. But it was great training and we came away with the green jersey for coming third overall. We completed this European stint with a third in the tandem road time trial at the 2011 Segovia (Spain) World Cup.

All this training made us very fit. When we went to the AIS in Canberra for testing, I had the blood pressure of an 18-year-old at age 40 while 20-year-old Scott's blood pressure matched his age exactly. However, the much lighter framed Scott impressed me by just outdoing me on the leg press.

In December 2011, Kieran was named the SASI Athlete with a Disability of the Year by the South Australian Sports Institute, along with Scott. It had been a great year for Kieran, but major problems lurked around the corner in the new year.

I've probably had about a dozen nasty crashes over my cycling career, most of them when out training and, strangely, mostly in the latter years. In most cases, it has happened when cars have turned in front of me, either because they didn't see me or misjudged my speed. Another classic problem occurs in peak-hour traffic. When cars are banked up, they occasionally stop to allow oncoming vehicles access into a side street. Cyclists often can't see this going on and I've ploughed into the sides of a few cars crossing the traffic flow, thankfully always at low speeds.

I have broken my collarbone three times, and every time this has happened it has been on a training run, never in a race. The first time was when a four-wheel drive suddenly turned in front of me. I left a large dent in its door, but scored a broken collarbone. This break healed naturally.

The next time I broke my collarbone was during a triathlon. The organisers had placed large metal signs on stands in the middle of the road to direct the triathletes. I was happily chatting to another cyclist and didn't notice the pack dividing to move around one of these signs. I hit it full on.

The last time I came off and broke the same bone was on a training run with Scott in Denmark. We were there for the World Championships. I was following Scott on a single bike and we were only 2 km from the hotel after a 100 km ride. Scott ducked up a ramp, but there was a lip there. I hit the lip on an angle, the front wheel chattered along and fell away, and I came down heavily on my right side. X-rays showed that I had broken my collarbone, fractured my arm and damaged my ankle. So they flew me home before the championships had even begun and Scott used a wheelchair to shunt me from one flight to the next. The medicos hadn't picked up that I also had a fractured hip. The 32-hour flight was agony. I didn't have any pain relief and I could hardly walk when I got home. Kerry took me straight from the airport to Flinders Hospital. I felt bad that we had been flown across the world only to have to return without competing. The Australian officials flew us back business class – and I didn't get to enjoy it!

At Flinders Hospital they took more X-rays, pinned the collarbone, found a chipped bone in Kieran's wrist and put the arm in a half cast. The pelvis and ankle were left to heal naturally. He spent a month allowing all the fractures to heal before he could get back on his bike.

Kieran and Scott then flew across the Tasman Sea to the Oceania Para-Cycling Track Championships in Invercargill, New Zealand, to see how they were progressing. These championships brought together the best track para-cyclists from New Zealand, Australia, Japan and South Africa. They won their events but their times were down. They needed to improve to be competitive in London.

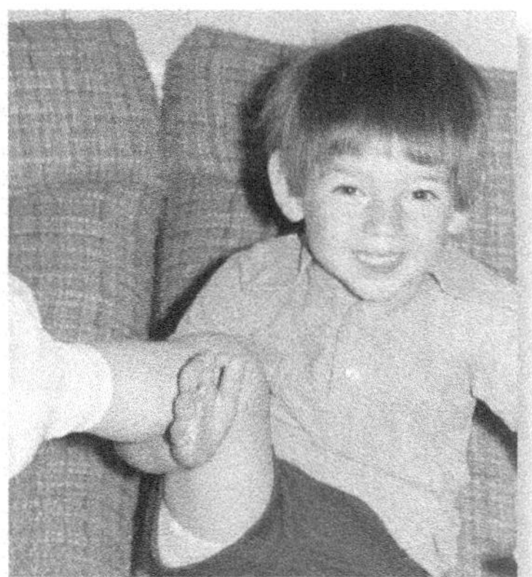

Kieran, aged two years, has probably just been to church ... he's wearing shoes. *Theo Modra*

As a little boy Kieran spent hours riding around the verandah of his Port Lincoln home. *Theo Modra*

Kieran enjoyed helping his dad by drenching sheep on Thistle Island, here in 1986 aged 14 years. *Theo Modra*

Kieran, 15 years old, wearing some of his 43 medals won at carnivals and championships all over Australia. *Theo Modra*

Peggy Bell, Kieran's wonderful housemother at Townsend House. *Andy Thurlow*

Katie, Peggy's dog, would follow Kieran around, fetch the frisbee and sit only on his lap. *Peggy Bell*

Winning the Under 19 pole vault in open company at the 1989 Australian All Schools Track & Field Championship in Adelaide was a major breakthrough for Kieran.

Coach John Hamann said the medal for winning the Under 19 pole vault was Kieran's biggest sporting achievement.

Winning a gold in the javelin at the 1992 national titles meant Kieran could now compete at the Seoul Olympics. *Theo Modra*

Kieran wheel-chaired Kerry around the 1996 Atlanta Paralympic site and they found some relief under the misting machines. *Theo Modra*

Under the circumstances, their Atlanta victory was a crowning moment and a tribute to Kerry's courage. *Theo Modra*

Hubert Opperman ('Oppy') is said to have designed this 'Side by Side' bicycle or 'sociable'.

Kerry and Kieran were married in St Stephen's Lutheran Church in Adelaide in 1997. *Theo Modra*

Kieran and Kerry both received an OAM from South Australian Governor Sir Eric Neal in 1997 for services to sport. *Theo Modra*

Kieran opens Tunarama. *Theo Modra*

Peter and Erika Kaesler designed and constructed their 'back-to-back tandem' (and trailer) and because it is collapsible, have ridden it all over the world. *Peter Kaesler*

Stamps featuring Australian sportspeople were released prior to the 2000 Sydney Olympics and Paralympics. *Theo Modra*

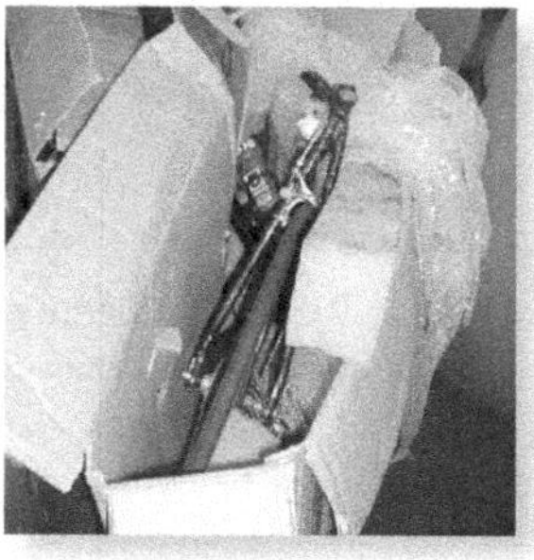

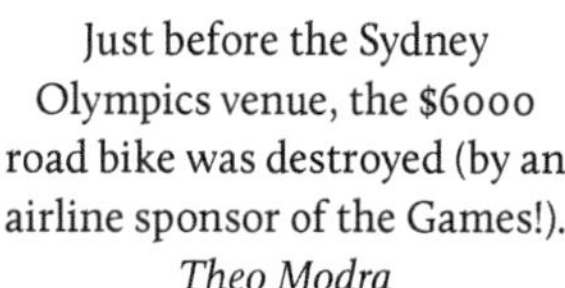

Just before the Sydney Olympics venue, the $6000 road bike was destroyed (by an airline sponsor of the Games!). *Theo Modra*

Kerry and Kieran have just missed, by a fraction of a second, a ride-off for a medal in Sydney in the pursuit.

Sarnya Parker and Kieran's sister, Tania, won gold at the Sydney Paralympics.

David Short, Robert Crowe and Kieran were still out of the Australian team for Athens, but they continued to train ... and smile.

Kieran with his beloved Nana (Dora) Modra. *Theo Modra*

Many of Kieran's clan, mostly his cousins, gathered in 2002 for his nana's funeral. *Theo Modra*

Simon (Tania's husband), Sylvia (Kieran's mum), and Tania were surprised to see him at the Athens Paralympic velodrome in 2004. Kieran, David and Robert were somewhat surprised to be there as well! *Theo Modra*

Despite multiple crashes, Robert Crowe, David Short and Kieran all got to win gold in Athens in 2004. Kieran can barely walk, but you can't wipe away that golden smile. *Theo Modra*

Robert Crowe can make it difficult for Kieran to concentrate. *Theo Modra*

Happiness is a welcome home parade.

Kieran's wonderful parents Theo and Sylvia were there once again for support when Tyson Lawrence and Kieran won gold at the 2008 Beijing Paralympics. *Theo Modra*

Kieran's daughters, Janae, Makala and Holly, with Kieran's favourite medals – the Beijing jade gold and bronze medal. Makala so wanted Kieran to win silver to make a set. *Theo Modra*

Australian Paralympic Committee President Greg Hartung with Libby Kosmala and Kieran, when they were both awarded the President's Medal for Excellence in Sportsmanship at the Paralympian of the Year awards in 2012. *Theo Modra*

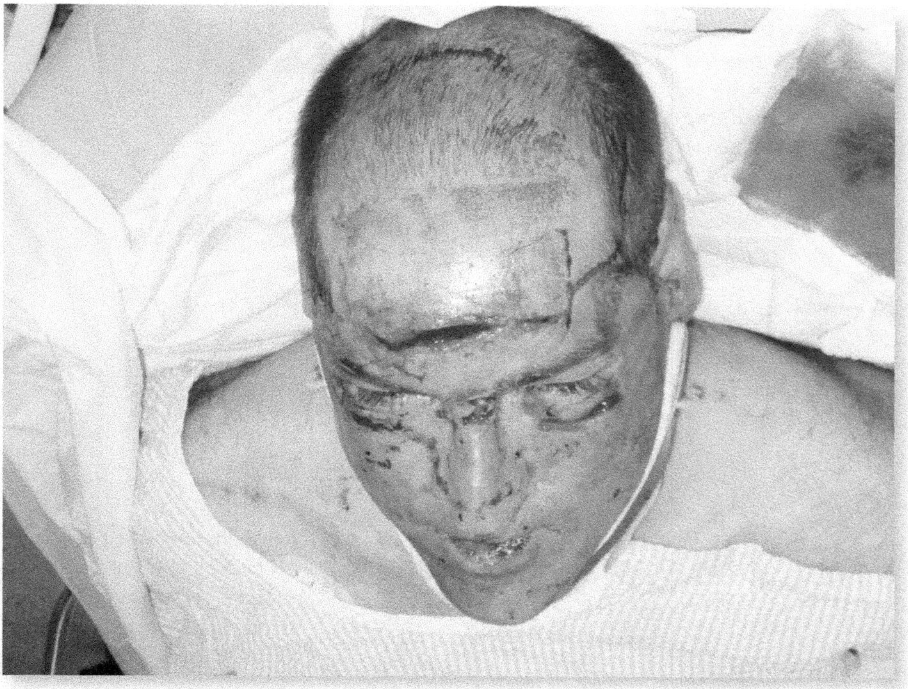

This is the photo that Kerry couldn't take. Kieran needed about 160 stitches after hitting a car in December 2011 and received bonus plastic surgery as a result. *Chris Golding*

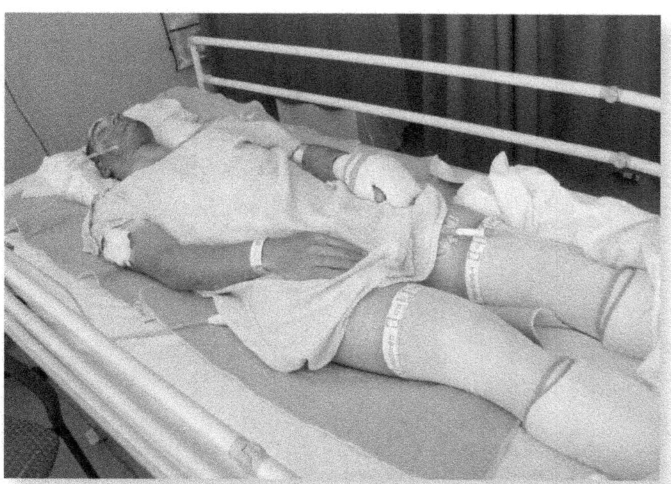

After being stitched and cleaned up, Kieran was kept in a brace and forbidden to move for ten days. *Chris Golding*

Kieran always appreciated a lovely note from home from his family. *Kerry Modra*

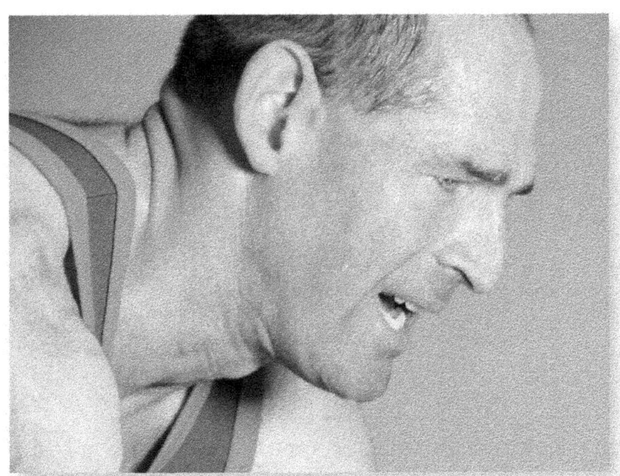

Rehabilitation wasn't easy but Kieran told the nurses, 'I've broken my back. I've broken my neck. Now I plan to break the world record!' *Theo Modra*

Kieran with Scott McPhee, their gold medals and a London bobby. *Theo Modra*

Kieran is the special guest speaker at the induction of new Sports Hall of Fame members at Immanuel College in 2012. *Theo Modra*

A friend, Mike Williams, invited Kieran to try kite surfing. Kieran noted how surprised Mike was when he took up the offer. *Theo Modra*

It was exciting tandem racing against Scots Neil Fachie and Craig MacLean at the 2014 Glasgow Commonwealth Games. Kieran and Jason pride themselves on being good sports, despite the disappointment.

Kieran spoke at a fundraiser for the Tandem Project in Adelaide in 2015. *Andy Thurlow*

Kieran, Darren, Sylvia, Theo, Mark and Tania at Theo and Sylvia's golden wedding anniversary in September 2015. *Colin Gill*

Makala, Holly, Janae, Kerry and Kieran at Theo and Sylvia's golden wedding anniversary in Kieran's local church hall. *Colin Gill*

Kieran and David Edwards won the pursuit at the national titles in Adelaide and got the chance to go to the world titles – and then maybe Rio. *John Veage/Cycling Australia*

Sprint racing is tight. *John Veage/Cycling Australia*

Mick Curran, Matt Formston (aka Oz Tandem), David, Kieran, Lachlan Glasspool and Kieran Murphy standing on the dais in Adelaide. *John Veage/Cycling Australia*

The ticket to Rio was presented by chef de mission for the Paralympics team, Kate McLoughlin.

Kieran took a selfie with David at a practice session. David's thigh was still healing. *Kieran Modra*

Kieran and David won an unexpected bronze for Australia in the 2016 Rio time trial.

They were very proud bronze medallists and totally 'over the moon'.

Kieran enjoys riding with the Tandem Project team. This promotional ride in 2016 was to Mt Jagged Wines, on the Fleurieu Peninsula between Willunga and Victor Harbor.

9 London and the hatchback

2012–2013

Only two weeks after returning to Australia from New Zealand, I was on my way to work. It was December; the roads were busy and I was riding my bike in heavy morning traffic. I normally ride along South Road; Brighton Road is generally busier and doesn't have a designated bicycle lane. But on this particular morning I took the more scenic Brighton Road. I slowed where the road narrows for traffic lights. I tend to ride out a bit to avoid getting too close to the gutters but I ploughed into a car parked in front of me.

It was fortunate that one of the girls who works with Kieran arrived at the crash scene shortly afterwards. She stopped the traffic, rang for help, phoned Kerry and sat with Kieran until the paramedics arrived. Kieran can't remember a lot of what happened, but Kerry does:

> Apparently when Kieran gained consciousness, his first words were: 'Don't tell my wife Kerry!' He still had his bag on his back and the paramedics cut it off. I know that this would have devastated Kieran and I can imagine him lying there and trying to keep the paramedics away from his bag!

Those that went to the accident scene later noted that there were roadworks in the area. Nobody came forward as a witness to what happened. Kieran was taken to Flinders Medical Centre where he was immobilised in a brace for ten days due to spinal injuries, including a compound fracture to the L4 vertebra.

While I was lying in hospital I became depressed. This was quite possibly a combination of the drugs, minor brain damage received in the crash, and the uncertainty about what was happening around me and the nature of my injuries. I began to really fear the nights, when I would have to deal with the pain and just wait for morning to arrive. I needed and got constant encouragement from family and friends.

Kerry had never seen Kieran so down, and this only began to improve when he could get up, use a walking frame and start his rehabilitation:

> I think it was worse for the girls and me. Kieran is a difficult person to slow down. Lying so still for ten days was absolute torture for him – and for us too. He is always so positive and we had never seen him so sad and lonely. Once Kieran could get out of bed, he was totally focused on rehab, getting back on his bike and London. We were worried about what might happen if he had another accident, missed out on London and maybe couldn't ride again.

Transferred from the hospital to Daw Park Repatriation Centre, I was moving from depression towards frustration. It was very hard learning to walk again and especially trying to keep my balance. I was in the ward with stroke victims and I kept challenging my physiotherapists. I wanted to do more and would keep exercising when they left. Nobody had touched my back and it was all knotted up. Later I found out that the physios didn't want to touch it until they got the all clear from the surgeons. I borrowed a tennis ball from the physios and tried to loosen it up by rolling it between my back and the wall.

My training regime was an hour with the physios, followed by an hour in the small repatriation centre's gym, mainly on the ergometer, and then an hour on a Wii board, hanging on to my frame and playing games to improve my balance. My biggest issue was not to do too much.

I had been awarded Para-athlete of the Year, and as I was on my back recovering my pilot Scott went to the presentation breakfast on my behalf and brought the trophy to me at the repatriation centre. Scott visited me all the time and would do whatever he could to help. He was a terrific support. Scott must have been worried that he needed me to recover for him to realise his London dream. But he never mentioned this. At no time did he put pressure on me. I would tell the nurses, 'I've broken my back. I've broken my neck. Now I plan to break the world record!'

Understandably Scott is awed by Kieran's recovery:

> It is quite easy to ride with Kieran. He has great power, yet keeps the tandem very steady. Training for London is the hardest bike work I've ever done. I was shocked when I first saw Kieran in hospital. I've never had anyone around me with an injury like Kieran's. I'm convinced that most people would have taken months, even years to get through it. As soon as he was allowed to walk he was working in the repatriation centre gym for four hours a day. It was unbelievable.

While I was recovering, the Para-cycling World Championships took place in Los Angeles and Scott piloted Bryce Lindores to gold in the pursuit – so the Australian Paralympic Committee did have a backup plan.

In March, a mere three months after the accident, I was able to visit the South Australian Sports Institute, where I was carefully checked over before getting the all clear to get back on my bike. But my doctors at Flinders Medical Centre were not happy with this assessment and to make sure that recovery was complete, I was sent to the Australian Institute of Sport in Canberra for medical tests. The experts there tested and X-rayed everything and gave me a clean bill of health. My body was okay, providing I exercised with care. The AIS wrote up a plan, which the doctors accepted. Getting back on the bike was no problem for me. My mind was already there. I just needed to take it easy and build slowly towards sprinting. I was mostly frustrated in our gym watching my colleagues lifting weights, which I knew I could manage, but couldn't risk.

The opening of the Paralympic Games was 12 August – a mere five months, or 20 weeks away! To be ready I began to do a lot of gym work, which I quite enjoy. Most of this is about strengthening my legs and core. Of course, I need my legs to be powerful and the two pieces of equipment I use most are the leg lift and the leg press, but you need to be able to hold your upper body still on the bike, and for that you need a strong core.

The word 'core' is frequently used in sports training. All core muscles are used when you bend down, pick up a weight and lift it overhead. Your core includes the four muscles of the stomach that wrap like a belt around the midsection, the muscles of your lower back, your pelvic floor, and your hips. There are over 15 of these muscles, and they even include the diaphragm, a core breathing muscle.

Kieran regularly leg-presses 220 kg using one leg. Many gymnasiums have leg press equipment, but many don't carry a maximum weight capability anywhere near 220 kg (and most people can't move anywhere near that even using both legs).

The London Paralympics was to be my swansong, my seventh and final Games in a career spanning 24 years of elite competition. Beginning slowly, Scott and I set our goals and built towards our dream.

The APC's Paralympic Preparation Program was created when Sydney was announced as host of the 2000 Games. After Beijing, this body immediately set up a training base in Newport, Wales, to acclimatise and prepare athletes for the London Paralympics.

The team left Australia for this camp, again flying in a specially chartered plane. The Newport training facilities were excellent with the velodrome similar to the London track. The para-cyclists were creating interest and a crowd of around 200 people turned up to watch their training sessions, a first for Kieran.

The London Olympics had created an interest in our sport and I was excited to see the crowd. I went over and talked to the people watching. They were all very interested in the tandems and I wanted to help them know more about what was going on. We all had a bit of a laugh together. The coaches weren't so pleased. I think they saw the crowds as a distraction from the training schedule. In my case the coaches were obviously right, but I got a crowd cheer when I jumped on the bike for my next run.

Kieran was going for a 'three-peat' (winning three consecutive championships) in the 4 km pursuit, scheduled for the first day of competition.

My reputation for not always obeying the chef de mission's rules preceded me and it was Scott who was given responsibility for keeping me in line. Scott was half my age and people would ask if he was my son. I didn't like that much. The age difference was sometimes frustrating, but in some ways our roles were reversed. I had a reputation for wandering off and doing things I wasn't supposed to do, while the coaches knew that Scott was the sensible one.

Scott had cared for me throughout my recovery from a broken back. Not only was he a talented cyclist, but also a great carer. He would make sure that I got to the track and that I got safely home. He would fill out my forms and take me to the food hall and describe the menu.

Kerry has memories of pilots who were not as thoughtful:

> Many pilots just go to ride the bikes. Forgetting that they need to make their VI teammates aware of obstacles, we've seen blind people walked into walls, windows and doors by their pilots!

* * *

In many ways, the Australian public needed a morale boost. Australians are very proud of their sporting heritage. Boasting a very much smaller population compared to the major sporting nations (Australia ranks 50th of 196 countries by population), Australians continually 'punch above their weight' in most sports. When any analysis is done where the population of a country is divided by the medals gained, Australia (and New Zealand) are consistently at the top or close to the best performers.

The Australian Olympic Committee had wanted the Australian able-bodied athletes to finish in the top five, but instead the Aussies ended up tenth in the gold medal rankings and seventh in overall medals. This was the worst result since Barcelona in 1992 when Australia came home with only 27 medals, including seven gold. And this time the usually powerful swim team, which kicks off the competition, had disappointed. In Beijing, the swimmers had contributed 20 of the 46 medals, but in

London the Australian swimming team won only 10 of the 35 won. This was Australia's worst Olympic swimming performance in 20 years and the Bluestone Review into this was quickly commissioned.

Interestingly, the AOC (Australian Olympic Committee) had predicted and benchmarked 35 medals in the lead-up to the Games, but its seven gold medals fell dramatically short of the 15 they had anticipated, based on 2011 World Championship results. Many Australians who had grown accustomed to international success were feeling let down, and in many ways the success of the Australian Paralympians filled that vacuum.

With few competition results in 2012 because of the accidents, Scott and I were first on the track to qualify – not a position we were used to. We had no idea what the others would do, so we had no choice but to go flat out and put our best time down.

As it turned out our time was good and to our surprise we qualified fastest. Five hours later and we were in the final. It is always a relief to get to race for gold. So many things can go wrong along the way, but once there, you can't take anything for granted. It still becomes your race and you must make sure that you cross the line before the other bike.

And Scott and I did. We won the 4000 m pursuit – the first Paralympic gold medal for Australia in London – and in a new world record time of 4:17.756 minutes.

I owe a great debt to Scott. He brought out the best in me. In fact, the accident has brought us closer together. Scott had really supported my progress and helped me through the rehabilitation stage to get back on my feet and get back on the bike again. If it had been anyone else, I wouldn't have been able to get back on the bike so quickly.

Kieran had won his third consecutive title in the event, beating teammates Bryce Lindores and pilot Sean Finning in the final. Bryce had enjoyed a successful career, but for much of the time had played second fiddle to Kieran. The Sydney Morning Herald *reported online Bryce's generous words following the event:*

> You can use it as a good benchmark or as a bit of a daunting one as you say, but Kieran's been around for years. He's an awesome bike rider and we look up to him and get ideas and thoughts off him and he is an awesome dude!

Ex-coach Kevin McIntosh was elated and relieved:

> Kieran has never had the optimal run into a major championship. It's a great bugbear. I wanted him to ride 4:11 in London. That was totally within his grasp. I wanted him to leave his mark on Paralympic cycling. I wanted him to walk away leaving something that was unattainable for years.
>
> When he had his accident, it was very difficult for me. I had talked him back into cycling and so I felt partly responsible and I struggled with that for a while. I struggled to go and see him and I have no idea why. To see him come through and be so successful was a great relief for me. It would have been devastating if it had ended his career and he wasn't able to achieve what was possible.

After winning gold, Scott and I were to struggle for success in our other events. We were 0.001 of a second behind the bronze medal time in the Kilo. Entered in the 24 km road time trial, our chain broke just off the start line, putting a quick end to our chances. We still had the road race over 104 km at Brands Hatch to go, but Scott got a severe dose of the flu the day before the race. We rode, but with Scott's illness getting worse, we pulled out three quarters of the way through.

In his closing speech, International Paralympic Committee President Sir Philip Craven described London 2012 as 'the greatest Paralympic Games ever'. With record crowds, numbers of broadcasters, athletes and countries taking part, combined with record-breaking performances from athletes and unprecedented media coverage, it was easy to see why.

Acting Prime Minister Wayne Swan was there to greet the Paralympians when they returned to Sydney. Australia's Paralympic team had arrived home from London with a haul of 85 medals, 32 of them gold. The team had medalled in nine of the 13 sports they competed in.

From very humble beginnings Paralympic sport had come of age and, in so many ways, Kieran had pioneered and contributed to this growth. Wayne Swan said on the team's arrival:

> Every single one of you has achieved a huge amount on the world stage of elite sport and we are enormously proud of your performances. Paralympic sport has well and truly hit a new level, with a record number of 4294 athletes from 165 countries and a global audience of up to 3.8 billion people.

Australia had come fifth on the medal tally table, a position the Australian public was more accustomed to. Since the inaugural event at Rome in 1960, Australia had finished among the top five, including a first place as host at Sydney and second in Atlanta behind the United States.

At the 2012 Paralympian of the Year Awards in November, Australian Paralympic Committee President Greg Hartung paid tribute to Paralympic legends Kieran Modra and Libby Kosmala (both South Australians), who were awarded the President's Medal for Excellence in Sportsmanship. This prestigious award, which recognises athletes who embody the values of respect, honour, fairness, modesty and integrity, has been awarded only twice before, to wheelchair racer Kurt Fearnley (2008) and alpine skier Toby Kane (2010).

Greg went on to say about Libby and Kieran:

> They are two of our most brilliant Paralympians whose individual successes at the Paralympic Games are exceptional and whose service to sport is admirable. Both have been involved in Paralympic sport for a long time and have watched it transform into the pinnacle of elite sport for athletes with a disability. With their years of experience, they are not only outstanding role models to their fellow team members but are outstanding representatives of the Paralympic movement.
>
> Kieran stands as one of the greatest athletes Australia has ever produced. With five gold and four bronze Paralympic medals, numerous world records and a Paralympic career that spans seven Games, three sports and medals in swimming and cycling, Kieran's commitment and passion for his sport is commendable.
>
> His enduring perseverance and pursuit of excellence was evident in London when he won gold in the 4 km individual pursuit with sighted pilot Scott McPhee. His third gold in the same event in three consecutive Games came less than ten months after a horrific accident in which he broke vertebrae in his neck and back. This was an achievement that reflected Kieran's resilience and his determination to overcome any obstacles and achieve his goals. To those qualities, he adds a modesty and sense of fair play that have made him one of Australia's great Paralympic champions.

The Kilkenny Cycling Club is very proud of Kieran's achievements as well. President Graham McArthur paid this tribute:

> He's a favourite son of Kilkenny and he's very well liked. Whenever Kieran's riding there's a good buzz about the club. Nobody knew he was legally blind when he started. His sense

> of what's around him is remarkable. When we worked it out we stopped him from riding solo and started talking to his Paralympic coach. We became a support mechanism to get tandem racing going for Kieran. He's just inspiring and when the kids find out what he's done, they're in awe.

Immanuel College, led by principal Kevin Richardson and board chairman Kym Wallent, had built a new state-of-the art aquatics centre on their school site in 2007. A wall of this building was dedicated to photos of ex-Immanuel sportspeople who have represented Australia at open-age level, and both Tania and Kieran feature. Among the many names in their 'Sports Hall of Fame' are Lleyton Hewitt, Don Lindner, Laura and Natalie von Bertouch, Jenny and Mark Williams and Kyle Chalmers. Kieran was invited to be the special guest speaker at the induction of new Sports Hall of Fame members in 2012, a great honour and a fitting way to cement a relationship with a school that supported him so well.

At the 2012 Channel 7–The Advertiser (South Australian) Sports Star of the Year awards, Anna Meares was recognised as the state's top athlete. Like Kieran, she had come back from a broken neck to defeat the previous queen of sprint cycling, Britain's Victoria Pemberton, to win gold at the London Olympics. At the awards presentation evening and among a galaxy of sporting stars, Kieran received the Tanya Denver Award for Endeavour and Sportsmanship.

In many ways, the London Paralympics was the fairytale ending to my sporting career. Lying immobilised in hospital I never thought I would have been able to do it. But you take things one step at a time and reinvent yourself. There is nothing better than to represent your country and be proud of your efforts. To stand up there on the podium and hear the anthem is exhilarating. But most of all it is very satisfying to see the training plans of four years come together to win gold and break a world record.

Kieran had retired and the speech at the President's Medal for Excellence in Sportsmanship presentation and the citation on that certificate was the ultimate honour.

But there was to be another twist. At the Commonwealth Games held every four years (between Olympic and Paralympic Games), cycling had been an optional sport. The host country had the right to include cycling in the sporting program or not, but there had never been any attempt to include para-athletes in any way.

This changed at the Manchester (England) Commonwealth Games in 2002, where the decision was made to include a number of para-sports in a fully inclusive sports program. Ten events across five different para-sports were selected; para-cycling was not one of them.

The number of events and para-athletes increased through the ensuing Commonwealth Games. For the Glasgow Commonwealth Games of 2014, there were to be more medal events for the para-athletes. Sir Philip Craven (President of the International Paralympic Committee) was delighted:

> It is tremendous news that Glasgow will host more para-sport events than at any other previous Commonwealth Games and this underlines the growth and popularity of para-sport at all levels. To have 22 medal events included in the Games in 2014, just two years after London, will ensure that Commonwealth athletes can continue to perform on the big stage in front of thousands of spectators.

And to the delight of the para-cycling fraternity, the Glaswegians included the men's 1000 m time trial B tandem and the men's sprint B tandem. The Australian Paralympic Committee now had to look for suitable competitors. Mmm ... Kieran Modra? Kerry had seen it coming.

> When they returned from London, the Paralympians attended a civic reception at Adelaide Town Hall. This was followed by celebrations, interviews and photographs as the happy group walked through Rundle Mall. At the Welcome Home ceremony the Australian team manager had approached me and told me about the upcoming tandem event at the Glasgow Commonwealth Games. He told me that they would put no pressure on Kieran who had retired, but he might be interested! They took us out for lunch. We knew what was coming. After the lunch, they did give us time to think about it, but it didn't take Kieran long to accept the challenge.

Once again, a pilot was selected and there was to be no tandem pursuit in Glasgow. This time it had to be a sprinter, Jason Niblett. I was ready for a change anyway.

When asked by the press about his new move into sprinting, Kieran told them that he had been pursuiting for three (Paralympic) Games and although he had done well in all of them, he felt he needed something to spice up the sport a little.

Sprinting is dramatically different, but to be a good tandem rider, you need be good right across the board. I do have a sprint background from when I first started; I did everything – sprint and endurance. But that was something like 15 years ago. I just needed to get back that sprinter mentality.

Jason Niblett was 30 years of age and had retired after missing selection to the London Olympics. He had been an outstanding junior and had won a team sprint gold at the Indian Commonwealth Games in Delhi in 2010. Jason was also based in South Australia and the pair set about trying to ride the very fast qualifying times.

I was aware of compromises and changes I would need to make. The biggest factor to help our team dynamics was Jason's enthusiasm. It was a bit of a learning curve for both of us. I needed to respect his background in sprinting, because I was not a true sprinter. My sprint was a little more endurance based, whereas his was raw power. There was a little bit of a clash: he was faster and stronger, but I would last that bit longer. But it was a good thing. It was a matter of weighing up our strengths and putting them together to make a package.

Our first big test came at the 2014 Para-cycling Track National Championships in Darebin, Melbourne. In the flying 200 m used to seed sprinters, the Australian selectors had set a qualifying standard of 10.4 seconds. We cracked this mark with a 10.1, meaning we were off to the Worlds and to the Commonwealth Games. We went on to win the sprint title.

The Kilo was next and on a sweltering 40-degree day we scorched around the four laps in a time of 1:03.134 secs, just outside my Australian record of 1:03.120 secs, to win that as well. Although we had shaved three seconds off our previous best as a new combination, we just missed out on the qualifying time.

After the race, Kieran spoke to the media:

> It was a big improvement out there for us today. I have no doubt we will get it (qualifying time), but we must work harder. We still have the World Championships and we will just keep using the stepping stones along the way.

When Cycling Australia announced the Australian Para-cycling Track Team for the UCI Para-cycling World Track Championships to be held in Aguascalientes, Mexico, from 10 to 13 April 2014, they added:

> South Australia's five-time Paralympian Kieran Modra headlines the team, with the three-time reigning four kilometre individual pursuit Paralympic gold medallist to partner former Australian sprinter Jason Niblett in the tandem sprint and time trial. The new pairing claimed two gold medals at the recent National Championships in Melbourne and will be looking for a solid performance in Mexico ahead of the Glasgow 2014 Commonwealth Games.

It is exciting when host nations introduce more and different para-sports to complement their able-bodied program. Do host nations introduce events in which they have a reigning champion or an excellent chance of winning a gold medal? Perhaps this question is rhetorical. At the 2012 London Paralympics the English won the two para-cycling events that were introduced in Glasgow. British para-cyclist Anthony Kappes won gold at both the Kilo and the sprints at Beijing, and then won the sprints again in London. His 10.050 was a world record qualification time for the Flying 200. He was only a year younger than Kieran. A Scottish rider, Neil Fachie, won the Kilo at London in 1:01.351 and came second to Kappes in the sprints. Fachie would be 30 at the Glasgow Commonwealth Games and in his prime. Why didn't the Glasgow organisers introduce Kieran's favourite event, the pursuit? Like all countries organising events, they played to their strengths. Asked at the time by the media about his chances, Kieran was more circumspect:

> I am nervous about Glasgow. I am sprinting again and with a new pilot. We will be up against new and different opposition and facing new challenges. My biggest fear is losing. I have come to expect to win. I know our times at present will probably get us a medal in Glasgow. Riding at the Worlds in Mexico will give us a much better idea and the altitude training there will be a bonus.

Jason was an accredited cycling coach at the South Australian Sports Institute (SASI) and therefore not only my tandem partner, but also my coach. I was happy with this arrangement. The only other time this had happened was in Rome before the Athens Games, when Rob Crowe and David Short took over as my coaches because we had been removed from the Australian team. Having new pilots helped me reinvent myself. The problem with being in a sport for such a long time is that you can get stale and lose the enthusiasm and the adrenalin rush. Jason brought fresh and modern ideas and techniques. I'd been tandem racing far longer than him, so he often asked me for advice.

It was difficult to maintain enthusiasm about track work. I have been around the velodrome track thousands of times and I got frustrated with the start-stop-start-stop routine, and resting in between efforts. I knew interval training was beneficial, but it was nice to get out on the road and ride for a couple of hours. Road work builds necessary endurance and it was important for me to have a balance between the two.

The question remained. Could Kieran convert to sprinting well enough to beat the Scots on their home turf?

10 … and other things

In the 2014 Australia Day Honours Kieran was made a Member of the Order of Australia 'for significant service to sport, as an athlete representing Australia at Paralympic Games, and to people who are blind or have low vision'. Already the recipient of an OAM (Medal of the Order), he could now add an AM (Member of the Order) to his name. This award was more special still, with only 340 members appointed in any calendar year. At the time Kieran was keenly involved with SPARC (Sports, Arts and Recreation Council) where he was paid to talk as a member of an outreach team, be a role model for people with disabilities, and show those in need where to find assistance and what was possible. He also volunteered with Blind Sports SA and Cycling SA's Novice Cyclist Program and was an ambassador for the South Australian Premier's 'Be Active Challenge'. Kieran was also part of a team that created the Tandem Project, a venture that trains vision-impaired riders to be competent tandem riders. He remains involved in many of these.

The AM tribute was very moving. It is the second medal that I haven't had to train for. My Order of Australia was the only other one. When I received news of my AM I wanted to share the presentation with Scott, who was honoured with an OAM on that same day. He was overseas racing in Europe, but after waiting for eight months, I regretfully had to accept it without him.

The AM means so much because it is recognition from the wider Australian community. I would put it alongside standing on the top of a podium. It is a great honour. I didn't quite know what to expect when I received it, but I am moved when so many people pass on positive comments and congratulations. Some of my cheekier friends have asked, 'Do we call you Sir now?' Sir Kieran Modra? Lady Kerry Modra? It does have a certain ring to it!

David Baker, joint managing director of the large Adelaide firm Baker Young Stockbrokers, is one of Kieran's greatest supporters. As the then President of Australian Paralympic Committee of South Australia, he was on the board of the APC. David is an ambassador speaker for men's health, receiving written commendation from Australian Prime Minister John Howard for his support for Australian Paralympic athletes. He was also a Foundation Member of the Adelaide Football Club and has a black belt in taekwondo. After witnessing Kieran's achievements firsthand, it was often David who would ring Kerry in Australia at all hours (usually very early in the morning), full of excitement and enthusiasm, to update her.

In 2013 David wrote to the Australian Honours and Awards Secretariat at Government House in Canberra, recommending Kieran for an Order of Australia award:

Dear Sir,

Kieran Modra is a model human being. Impaired vision has not deterred this fellow. He puts such energy into whatever he pursues, whether it be for others, charity or himself.

His record as a Paralympian speaks for itself. It's on record – all 24 years of it!

A veteran of seven Paralympic Games, he represented Australia in javelin, swimming and cycling, from Seoul in

1988 to London in 2012. A five times Paralympic gold medalist, Kieran is one of the most decorated and respected members of the Australian Track Cycling Team – a pioneer in tandem cycling.

What's not on record is his dedication to the cause of impaired vision, where he is so determined to help and make a difference to those who have suffered, as he has all of his life.

Personally, in his own drive for excellence, in his pursuit of gold in the London Paralympics, he rode himself into selection by winning the Nationals with just eight weeks of training. Then, at around Christmas time, nine months before the Games, he had a horrific accident, leaving him in hospital undergoing rehabilitation for approximately three months. I spoke with him during this time. On his back, with his neck in a brace, he was asked the question, 'What about London?' He looked at me and smiled, signalled with a finger and said, 'I'll take gold.' This was an impossibility as far as his doctors and I were concerned.

The rest is history. He won gold and broke his own Paralympic and World record – a champion athlete – a champion individual.

It is with the greatest pleasure for me to be part of the Reference Team for Mr Kieran John Modra OAM to be considered for an award within the Order of Australia.

I have known Kieran since the year 2000 (the year of the Sydney Paralympic Games) and since that time we have worked closely in the pursuit of his dreams. A number of times he has brought tears of joy to those he has addressed publicly, and to individuals about his life on a bike and his imagination of sight. He has used his success by sharing with others, whether able bodied or disabled, that life is a treasure and we should never forget it.

He is the perfect example of what an ambassador for disability should be, and worthy of any award that should be bestowed upon him.

In my capacity as President of Australian Paralympic Committee, South Australia, and as a person who has witnessed first-hand the attributes of this man, I feel honoured and privileged to have met him, watched him and worked with him. I feel like I am part of his family. I am one of his greatest supporters.

Should you require further information or have any questions please do not hesitate to contact me.

Yours sincerely
David R. Baker

* * *

In our more private lives away from sport, Kerry and I have faced and overcome many hurdles. We are certain that the accident before the London Games has caused me a loss in short-term memory, more headaches and lower back pain issues. And there is the challenge of money and financial security.

Thankfully governments and sponsors have allocated and contributed increasingly larger sums of money and support to para-athletes, para-sport and the Paralympic movement. Because Kieran is an elite athlete he received financial assistance from the government in grants and scholarships from Cycling Australia, and he has received a disability pension since the age of 16. This, however, is not a sufficient or sustainable income stream for a family.

For many years I was the part-time Sport and Fitness Development Officer at Townsend House and worked three days a week as a mentor for students. The South Australian School for Vision Impaired (SASVI) had set up units that catered for visually impaired students at targeted secondary schools. Seaview High was one of those and I worked with a vision-impaired (VI) boy who was struggling to integrate into high school life. I sat with him in all his classes and encouraged and helped him wherever I could. Because he didn't want to appear different, he didn't use his vision aids. But I do and the other kids then think it's okay. I encouraged him to join my tandem program and he is learning how to make friends.

My employer generously paid me while I was at championships or trials nationally and overseas. Kerry had given up her job to look after our children.

Finding work is not easy. I have seen a transition from little awareness of vision impairment, to the situation now, where I feel there is almost too much. It is difficult for people like me to get employment. Employers need productivity, and vision-impaired people are generally slower at doing most tasks. There are laws that protect employees, and rightfully so, but they do make employers cautious when considering employing someone with a disability.

Kieran's concern about the prospects of finding employment was borne out by the results of a 2016 UniSA study of hundreds of South Australian employers. It found that only 37% had hired people with disabilities, despite them having positive feelings about doing so. The leading author of the report, Dr Liz Hemphill, noted that besides the larger risk of including people with disabilities in their workforce, there was a fear of the cost of workplace alterations and customer and workforce reactions.

* * *

We have three girls. Little was known about optic atrophy when the girls were born and I was assured that my condition was most likely a genetic accident. Holly, our eldest, was born in 2001 and we share a birthday. At birth the doctors told us that her eyes were fine. When she was four years old and attending kindergarten, we noticed that she would get lost. In the park, she would sometimes go to the wrong person. Tested again, it was discovered that she had juvenile optic atrophy – and very similar in degree to my condition.

Makala was born two years after Holly and her juvenile optic atrophy was diagnosed when she was three-and-a-half. She has only five degrees of her peripheral vision and night blindness, making it even more difficult for her. To make tasks like crossing the road possible, she is learning how to scan; checking each way in small head movements to get the total picture.

There are very few cases of optic atrophy in the world and most of the information comes from studies overseas. Kieran is one of the few adults in South Australia with this condition. Researchers in England are testing his DNA to try to isolate the culprit gene. Surprisingly, while a troublesome gene has been discovered to be the cause of optic atrophy in 75% of known cases, this gene is normal in his genetic code. The experts want to test the girl's DNA as well, but they will only do this after they have identified Kieran's problem.

Holly was legally blind at four and so was enrolled in the South Australian School for Vision Impaired (SASVI) in Ascot Park, a southern suburb of Adelaide. Makala's sight was not severe enough for her to gain entry until Year 2. In the meantime, she struggled academically and emotionally at her first primary school, as her sight deteriorated at a quicker rate than either Holly's or Kieran's.

To assist our vision, Holly, Makala and I use a range of devices: monoculars, video magnifiers (also known as closed circuit television systems or CCTVs), hand-held or stand magnifiers, screen reading computer programs (like 'Jaws'), and iPads. Makala uses binoculars. We have all been supplied with white canes. There have been monumental advancements in vision aids over my lifetime. When my vision problems were identified, the teachers at Townsend taught me how to use the monocular scope and a large magnifying glass, which we called a dome. They knew that touch-typing would be crucial, so we learned on old mechanical style typewriters. We were all very excited when a primitive computer was bought by the school. These were the only aids I had, and while they are still useful, I am amazed at the technology that Holly and Makala can access.

Our third and youngest daughter, Janae, was born in 2005 without optic atrophy, but with Tetralogy of Fallot (TOF), a heart condition that results in low oxygenation of the blood and therefore fatigue and retarded growth. We were unaware of this until we took Janae to a doctor when she was 11 months old suffering from a persistent cold. We were in for a shock. The doctor checked for bronchitis and heard a heart murmur. Janae was immediately transferred to hospital and three weeks later was having open-heart surgery in Melbourne! It was stressful and scary, but we are so thankful that they heard the murmur and operated so quickly.

Since then Janae has had a stent inserted to widen her narrow pulmonary arteries and in 2013 the specialists removed that stent, patched it and repaired a pulmonary valve. She has missed a lot of school over the years, but is now putting on weight, growing taller and feeling far better and more energetic.

All three girls have struggled with friendships. Schools have tried hard to integrate them into mainstream school life. Like me at a younger age, they are sensitive to comments from peers and lacking in confidence. In their own way and time they are coming to terms with their disabilities. Like any younger person, they do not like to be different.

Kerry often muses over a classic dilemma:

> When the VI children go to SASVI they get more individualised attention from teachers who are experienced and trained to work with this handicap. However here they are socialising with a small group of children who have similar problems, so they need to be integrated into the larger world. But when they are moved into mainstream and usually much larger classes, with teachers who are coping with a wider range of challenges, their education suffers.

The family all miss meeting with other parents and children who are coming to terms and coping with problems similar to theirs. Kerry, especially, misses the friendships:

> We don't get together with other parents as much as we used to. Can:Do 4Kids was good at initiating this and ran programs and special days to get us all together, but that has stopped. VI children get picked up at their school and brought home by taxi, so parents don't see and meet up with each other at the school like many other parents do.

After trying her first choice of basketball, Holly started cycling competitively, and with some success. As a 12-year-old she did very well at the Australian Para-Cycling Road Nationals in 2012, winning the open time trial over 21.8 km with pilot Victoria Veitch in a time of 44 minutes (44:15.0), and an average speed of 35.9 kph. Holly loved it:

> I trained for six months and then went with the whole family to Echuca for the meet. The time trial was over 21 km and we won that. The road race was four laps of the same time trial course, but because of my age the officials would only let me do one lap. Victoria and I had a plan. We wanted to be in front after our first and only lap, but the crank on my end of the

> tandem broke early on. I would like to do more cycling, but now I am getting used to high school and all that homework.

We are proud of her results, but conscious of not adding extra expectations and pressure. Her motivation needs to come from an enjoyment base. Holly is going to try some other sports and then she will know if she wants to keep on cycling.

Holly was a little unsure of herself when moving from a primary school of 40 students to a secondary school of around 400. She has always been interested in animals, particularly horses, and her bedroom is festooned with horse ornaments of all shapes and sizes. Kerry has noticed a big change:

> Since Holly has gone to high school, she is asking questions like: 'When I'm a mum, how will I cope with my baby? How will I be able to see what my baby is doing? How do I put makeup on?' She will need to work through these issues and, like Kieran, she will.
>
> Makala is more quiet and sensitive. She likes routine and the surety of familiar surroundings, and is good at art, especially drawing. She loves her extracurricular art lessons and her bedroom is full of her pictures.
>
> Janae likes drama and acting and has a bubbly personality, but this was sorely tested during the trauma of heart surgery. Our children all enjoy the family trampoline, although I am always on stand-by with the first-aid kit. Our trampoline was bought with all of the safety requirements. It was the deluxe model with netting and padding everywhere. We thought it was bullet proof, but our girls managed to break arms, ankles and wrists on it! Gradually the netting and padding perished and since then we have had no accidents. The girls love being on it and we often see them just lying out there and reading books.

Like most girls of their age, our girls enjoy playing electronic video games. I enjoy occasionally joining them on the Wii. The girls all have their own hand-held electronic consoles, bought initially by us to make car travel easier. Kerry and I were in for a surprise. Driving longer distances has always been a challenge. Maybe this is a normal family problem, but when three in the car can't see out properly, impatience grows, niggling starts, tempers fray and no one can enjoy the experience. So when we bought the individual electronic consoles, we thought we were in for more peaceful cruising. The girls soon found out that by using Wi-Fi they could link up their consoles and play against each other. We think that sometimes their arguments are now even worse!

Visually impaired people need space. We need to be able to put items on surfaces so that we can find them again. We need space for our special equipment. However, finances are tight and we live modestly in a smallish home in Hallett Cove. After living with Kerry's parents for a year, we bought a home in Morphett Vale in 1997 and then our present home in 2001. We don't have a mortgage or owe money and I do my best with my woodworking skills to maintain and improve internal fittings. It's been a struggle but we've lived within our means. Cycling is an expensive sport, so we've had to prioritise. We don't have a lot of modern conveniences and we would like to be closer to Adelaide and on the flat. But we can't afford that and need to extend our home instead. Our kitchen needs improvement as well. I enjoy woodwork and have built our verandah and some of our furniture. When I tackle these projects, Kerry says she likes my 'rustic look' and I'm still uncertain if that is a subtle suggestion that my woodworking skills could be better.

Kerry and Janae are the eyes for our family. Kerry laments that three members of her family can never find anything. I am one of the worst. I'm not very tidy. I've got the best of intentions, but things get stacked and I spend a lot of time foraging around trying to find things. It's very frustrating for me, but it must be very difficult for Kerry and Janae to see us hunting for something that is right in front of us!

I can drive but I'm not allowed to drive on public roads, so Kerry has to drive the family anywhere and everywhere. This makes it difficult for activities after school and sport. Kerry has to herd us when we go shopping together, and if during the day she changes her hairstyle or clothes, we have difficulty recognising her.

Supermarkets present unique challenges for Kerry:

> Shopping can be an interesting experience. If I send the girls off to get something and if they are not careful, they will drop it into another shopper's trolley by mistake. This must make for some interesting discussions when those people get to the checkout!

I am aware of the extra pressures put on Kerry. I think she has had it harder than me. I've grown up with it, but she came into it, and then had to adjust to the chaos that this brings into life.

* * *

Over my career, I have witnessed a huge change in the construction of bicycles and tandems. At the beginning of my para-cycling experience, I borrowed a tandem frame and bought and added parts so I could ride with Kerry. During the Sydney Paralympics, and since then, all equipment has been provided and there are specialised mechanics to tune my bikes. As cycling, and tandem cycling in particular, has become more professional, a lot of money and effort has gone into research and development of this equipment. My teammates and I are measured up to our tandems to maximise efficiency and performance, and the materials used for construction are constantly becoming lighter and stronger.

A question often asked is what goes faster, a bicycle or a tandem. In any comparison, we have to assume that both cycles are being ridden by cyclists of equal ability, and that the cyclists of the tandem pair are evenly matched and work well as a team.

It is easy to mount a good case for the tandem. It would appear to have twice the pedalling power, with only slightly more frictional loss in the drivetrain. Seemingly it has about the same wind resistance as a conventional bicycle. High-performance tandems may weigh less than twice as much as a single bike, so the power-to-weight ratio may be slightly better than that of a single bike and rider. It sounds like the tandem is winning the debate.

Yet current world records show that a single bike rider is over one second faster over 200 m, five seconds quicker over the Kilo, seven seconds superior over the 4000 m pursuit and travelled 7 km further when creating the one hour record.

Is it simply because a cyclist on a single bike can accelerate more quickly from a standing start?

Recent research in wind tunnels suggests there are many reasons. It has shown that the drag from a tandem is significantly greater than that of a single bike. Wind resistance is one thing, but the amount of air that the larger tandem pulls makes a single bike quicker. Although when looking at the frontal surface area of a tandem it may appear similar, the wind does not share this outlook. The second frontage of the stoker, the turbulent air pocket between the riders along with the increased length of the tandem all contribute to increasing the drag by a further 30% to 50%. It would not surprise me if at some stage a body suit is designed to somehow join the tandem riders and partly overcome this problem.

One would assume that the power output of two riders would double the power delivered to the bike. However, this doesn't bear out with testing. Recently a pair tested their maximum power individually on a wattbike and recorded the following outputs: Rider 1 = 1600 and Rider 2 = 1400 ... a total of 3000 watts. When this same pair tested their output on a tandem, they could only deliver 1900 watts to the rear wheel. A logical explanation of this may come from the length of the multiple stepped power transfer. The pilot's power needs to transfer through the timing chain before arriving at the drive chain before reaching its final destination – the rear hub. Each step allows a leakage of watts.

A third factor might well involve the co-ordination of the tandem riders. To achieve maximum efficiency, both riders need to be in sync. This might well explain why tandem teams with 'weaker' individual riders can outclass teams with two 'stronger' riders.

I have always been a proponent of teamwork and spend many hours with my pilot practising and improving technique. I acknowledge the speed superiority of a single bike, but there isn't a lot in those records and a lightweight frame carrying two powerful bodies is a fearsome missile. On the road, we often whistle past single bikes on a downhill run and can often pass them pulling up a hill. We have cyclists out on the road who love to tuck in behind us. They are dragged along in our suction and tell us it's a bit like riding behind a motorbike.

A whole cycle-building industry has developed around the rise in success and ensuing popularity of cycling in Australia. One person who has pioneered tandem construction is Daryl Perkins, a successful sprint, six-day and tandem rider. From 1970 until 1975 he raced in Europe, where the best bikes of that era were made in Italy. Like most cyclists of that era, he brought the Italian bikes home to Australia. After problems with his Italian bike this fitter and turner by trade was soon making his own frames in his parents' shed in Bentleigh, a Melbourne suburb. The father of another well-known Australian cycling champion, Shane Perkins, Daryl was on the cutting edge of bike building, using technology and specialised software to match up a cyclist's body measurements with the optimum bike, always aiming to maximise pedal power, balance and comfort, whilst minimising air drag. This all must be done without infringing rules about bike construction, set out and governed by the Union Cycliste Internationale (UCI).

Daryl came to watch us race in Melbourne and was amazed at the amount of twist in our bike frame. I was still riding the bike Scott and I used for the pursuit in London. During a standing start at training they measured Scott and my combined power output at 2500 watts. The champion British track sprinter Sir Christopher Hoy can achieve this kind of power, but not at the start, only during a race. The power generated by our combined weight of 150 kg pushing through the pedals can snap chains and frames easily. Jason had a bigger body than Scott and more raw power. We needed a stronger frame, and Daryl planned to wrap steel tubing in carbon fibre to achieve the strength without the weight.

Training methods are constantly changing. In the early days, I devised my own schedule when the first trainers and coaches believed that the most effective training programs involved intensive physical work over as long a time frame as possible. This approach has changed over time and the modern approach often confuses me. When Kerry and I were riding together, training was a case of just riding as hard as possible. A rest day happened when you couldn't ride any harder. Now I can't work out why people are having so much rest! What! *Another* recovery ride? My legs are feeling fine! But I had to accept a new training regime. This is and was extremely difficult, unlearning old training habits that had worked in the past. In my case I have had to pay more attention to three aspects: diet, recovery and developing good core stability. Everything is based on my power to weight ratio, so I need to manage my weight and yet have adequate levels of energy. The amount of sugar in foods is a growing problem and so I tend towards unprocessed food. Recovery is important. I used to always have tired legs. Allowing them to recover allows me to train at very high intensities. My upper body must be perfectly still while my legs are working flat out, so I work on building a good core. My exercises include 'planking' for four minutes – the duration of a normal pursuit race.

'The plank' is an isometric core strength exercise that involves maintaining a difficult position for extended periods of time. The most common plank is the front plank, which is held in a push-up position with the body's weight borne on forearms, elbows, and toes. It sounds easy. Please try it, and then have a go at holding it for four minutes.

Even the tracks have changed. They differ all around the world, but generally indoor velodromes are built with less expensive pine surfaces. Designers have been moving away from traditional materials. The 1996 Atlanta Olympics saw the introduction of synthetic surfaces supported by steel frames. All tracks are now 250 m in length, but they are quite different to ride. I like the Dunc Gray Velodrome in Bass Hill (north of Sydney) because it seems to have bigger bends.

* * *

Maybe surprisingly I like to tat and crochet. Both tatting (lace-making) and crocheting are age-old skills and taught to me by my grandmother and sister. When Nana Modra and Tania travelled to Port Lincoln from Adelaide to see me open Tunarama, I asked Nana to teach me tatting. After giving me instructions, she went off to visit a friend. When she returned and saw my work, she said, 'Kieran, if I were you, I would give that away.'

Sister Tania offered to show me, using a thick rope. I got the idea and can now tat skilfully to make doilies and centrepieces. I often tat when Kerry is driving, especially on long-distance trips. I have very fond memories of a close relationship with Nana. She has taught many people to tat, but very few have persevered to master the skill. I think she was almost shocked that despite my visual impairment, I was one. I really enjoyed visiting her to compare notes on our tatting. She inspired me and enjoyed my enthusiasm. As I got better at it and tried more and more complicated techniques and designs, I would look forward to showing her my efforts. My biggest achievement was a centrepiece with a diameter of 50 cm, needing 100,000 knots, a kilometre of thread and six months to complete. I don't have the time to do these sorts of projects now and unfortunately my nana is no longer with us. She was a wonderful friend and I enjoyed that extra connection that tatting provided.

I often tat on the long plane trips and it's a real conversation starter. Lots of people are interested to see someone doing this ancient craft and I'm often surrounded by spectators and flight attendants.

Making documentaries, especially from film footage taken on my many trips around the world, is another enjoyable hobby. Action shots enliven movies shots and this has brought me into conflict with most of my coaches. When I can, I take a camera out on the tandem. The heavy older cameras were nothing like the

GoPro-style cameras of today. Coaches don't like this. In fact, they hate it! They know I can handle these cameras, but are concerned the equipment might fall on the track. For safety, track cyclists cannot take anything onto a track that might fall off, including water bottles. I took a shoulder-style studio camera out on one occasion, but it was a closed track session and the coach was informed.

We don't go to cinemas or concerts often, but enjoy television. The TV cameras can get right up close to the action, so we can see what's happening more clearly. In our home the three of us with VI sit together less than two metres from a very big, widescreen TV. It's great if the remote is not working, or we lose it, because we can just reach out and manually change the channels or volume on the TV! James Bond and Doctor Who are two of my favourite characters.

Kieran's cottage mother Peggy remembers an incident when he was a 12-year-old and is pleased his taste in movies has changed:

> I trusted Kieran and asked him to go to the video shop and pick out a suitable movie, as I couldn't go. Well, they were on their second viewing before I walked through the TV room. Both boys' eyes were glued to the TV and mine nearly popped out of my head. Kieran had hired an R-rated movie. The two boys had their talk on sex education that night!

I like lots of different music genres and I probably listen more to the melody than the lyrics. I often use music to hype me up and I keep an ear out for what our girls are enjoying. I like instrumental music too, and use this as backing to movies of my trips, or action clips from bike riding and kite surfing. Kerry loves Christmas carols, but starts playing them a long time before Christmas Day and after a while it drives me bonkers. Kerry calls me a 'humbug' because I am reluctant to put up the Christmas decorations and lights too early. I'm feeling pretty clever this year, because I didn't take the lights down after last Christmas – they are ready to go.

Every now and then I will pick up and play my guitar. At Townsend House I learned to play the trumpet, piano and sing – but not all at the same time! My trumpet playing continued while I was at Immanuel College, as well as singing in the choir and performing solo work.

School principal Mike Williams invited me to try kite surfing. I think he was surprised when I accepted his offer. I asked him, 'To do this, what do I need to be able to see?' His interesting response was, 'I can't answer that, because I don't know what you can see.' So he taught me and we took it slowly and cautiously. I soon found out that although I can see the kite, I can't see the lines and tangling can cause problems. When I am setting the kite up and connecting lines, I check and double-check to make sure all is working. I never kite surf by myself and Mike is always around to help me out. The biggest problem I have is losing my board when I come off. If the board is 15 metres away, I struggle to see it and Mike will show me where it is. I tried an elastic board leash, but I have a scar (ten stitches long) on the back of my head to show where the board came back and whacked me!

My cousin Ben sold me my first kite and I soon had to make repairs. So I learnt to sew the spinnaker material used for kites and, before I knew it, I was fixing up kites for friends. So why not make one? I have now made two good-sized kites, each with an area of around ten square metres, and am presently making my third.

Completing a certificate in scuba diving has confused some people, who ask me why I bother when I can't see underwater.

Sometimes it's not only what you see, it's enjoying the atmosphere. I love the feeling of weightlessness and the water around me. As bad as my eyes are, I still often look over my shoulder for those big, grey fish with the sharp teeth!

People with disabilities rely heavily on public transport and I often travel long distances to training venues. Fortunately, Hallett Cove is well served with a regular bus and train network. I always give myself plenty of time to get to destinations. My parents were notorious for being late at functions – and they haven't changed. We always seemed to be running behind time and rushing to get to events. It's a habit I can't afford to have. I always leave myself time so that I don't put myself under pressure if things go awry, as they often do. Because I can't drive, I get a free public transport pass, but catching buses is one of the more difficult things to do. I can't see the travel route identification on the bus, so I need to hail them all. Understandably bus drivers get annoyed and I have been abused, but they are generally apologetic when they see my blind travel pass. If there are other people waiting, I'll often ask them what bus they are catching and then relax and just follow them on. I carry my white identification cane more now, and other travellers and bus drivers are usually helpful and considerate when they see that.

Sometimes I take one of my latest interests with me to cover the shorter distances – my unicycle! There were a few unicycles at Aldinga Primary. I thought the students might like to use them but I reckoned I needed to be able to ride one before I introduced them to the group. They also had 'spin sticks' at the school, which is a new form of juggling with sticks. I've learnt to do that too.

Kieran enjoys waterskiing, open-water scuba diving, kayaking and off-road mountain bike riding. His latest interest is in bees. Back on the home farm in Port Lincoln, Theo and Kieran are building up a nice collection of hives and extracting honey. Kieran has built many 'top-bar hives'. With a top-bar to support the comb, these hives are typified by removable frames, which allow the apiarist to inspect for diseases and parasites. Movable frames also allow a beekeeper to split the hive more easily to make new colonies.

My poor vision makes it very difficult for me to identify a queen bee, a necessity when creating a new colony. I can't get back to look after the bees as often as I would like and I would really enjoy having my own hive in our backyard. There is little space there and I might have to be content with my worm farm.

When I was much younger, I was dressed in my best clothes every Sunday on the farm and taken to church, where Mum and Dad were very involved. Christianity has stayed with me, but it hasn't been an easy task. There have been many factors that have influenced my faith. Moving at such a young age to Townsend House in Adelaide was probably the first real test. Townsend didn't have a specifically Christian focus, but they did support the ideology and my family's beliefs. At age 11 I would ride the three kilometres to the Warradale Lutheran church. I enjoyed the ride and the church. When I was 15, I did my confirmation studies there, but was officially confirmed, and thus allowed to take Holy Communion, in Port Lincoln by Pastor Rob Paech. At Townsend I learned to play the trumpet and piano, so I happily played with the church band. But I struggled with Christianity during those years. I always had the belief, but I was learning to live with my impairment. I blamed God for this extra problem. It just didn't make sense. It wasn't fair. As an adolescent I was feeling rebellious. And yet I believe my Christian faith helped me pull through that period of adjustment. When I started attending Immanuel I could relax. Here Christianity was the norm, with regular services, prayer groups and the like.

I can think of three other major factors that have challenged my faith and my attendance at church: Sunday sport, Kerry and travel. A lot of sport and training is now scheduled for Sundays and I need to meet these requirements, so I miss a lot of church for this. When I met Kerry, she didn't have a faith. She had attended various Sunday schools, but church wasn't a family thing for her. Christianity has been a struggle for her and I try to encourage it as much as I can. She is open-minded about religion and will attend church, but generally when we can go together, as a family. Lastly, I spend a lot of time away travelling with my sport. I am often interstate or overseas at championships or camps.

Now I can see that God has given me this gift. It was often difficult to see where I was going, but when I look back I can now appreciate God's involvement in my life's direction. When I was 13 I was asking: 'God! Why?' Now I can see how God is using me. We all have deficiencies. If we can work on these positively, we can make a difference. Blindness is a huge problem, but if you can come to terms with it and work with it, then you can hold your head high and be proud of who you are. It's been a long process, but now I pass my worries and concerns to God. I can say: 'Okay, this is how You made me. You've made me this way for a reason. Thank you for the love and for making me who I am.'

I like to challenge and help others to develop skills and achieve goals, and I am often called on to speak to groups as a motivational speaker. We have only one crack at life, so we need to fill it with determination, motivation and inspiration. We all have many talents, some are just undiscovered. Life is full of challenges and we all tackle these challenges differently. So keep pressing forward and find the support of people around you to motivate and inspire you to find your talents. I've lost more races than I've won, but to accept defeat and push on is what it's all about. As a blind person, there is little chance of ever becoming over confident. There is always that little voice in your head telling you to be careful. You can't quite see where you're going – but you go anyway.

Nick Dean has heard Kieran speak:

> Kieran is an excellent speaker. It's a bit like going to the movies. In a half-hour Kieran speech, you will feel all of the emotions that you get in a movie – from laughter to tears – and when he talks, he talks from deep down. He gets the message across, better than an able-bodied athlete. He's physically imposing and his voice matches that. He has a sense of humour, is always humble and is fearless. As far as the Paralympic movement goes, Kieran Modra is primary history in the modern Paralympic era. He's risen with it.

11 Mexico and Echuca

2014

The 17-member squad wrapped up its ten-day training camp at the Adelaide Super-Drome in early April, and flew to Mexico for the world titles, to battle over 100 of the world's best cyclists from 30 nations.

Located at an altitude of 1887 m in north-central Mexico, Aguascalientes has two velodromes and a long-standing experience in staging major track events. Built in 2009, the 250 m Bicentenary track was made from Finnish wooden Kerto laminate, which is widely regarded as a quick surface to race on. The circumference at the fence was measured at 285 m, making it sensible to ride as close to the bottom of the track as possible.

Aguascalientes means 'hot waters' in Spanish, originating from the abundance of hot springs in the area. The state was created in 1857 when it was separated from neighbouring Zacatecas. The story goes that the wife of the governor of the state promised to give a kiss to the President of the time in exchange for the separation of Aguascalientes from Zacatecas, which explains why the state has the shape of a kiss!

Kieran emailed his friends and family soon after arriving:

Things are going well. We've had a few teething issues, but all is good. The altitude is quite a challenge and we must be careful not to do too much too soon. We have started our intensity work and yesterday snapped the chain on a start

> for an effect. We have fixed the problem, I hope! The other countries are rolling in and the track training sessions are getting increasingly busier. My first race begins on Friday with the Kilo, the sprint is on Sunday. The Mexican food is good; hot but good. The traffic is crazy. I don't know where to look, left or right or at the red light. Foot-high (30 cm) kerbs means you must watch your step. Anyway, I'm looking forward to it all.

Some of the initial teething issues were caused by the bespoke Perkins frame.

A lot of money was spent on the frame to make it stronger using carbon fibre and Kevlar. Although slightly heavier than the Perkins frame we used in London, it was stiffer and that generally means better. When a frame flexes you are losing energy, it is harder to steer and because the cogs need to stay in line, there is a tendency for the chain to slip off. We were looking forward to riding this brand-new Perkins tandem, but at high intensity we developed a speed wobble, which possibly had something to do with the geometry of the design. We wanted to persist with this new frame, but we just didn't have the time. At the top end of the track we hit speeds of 68 kph. When the bike wobbled there, we knew it wasn't safe to sweep down the track at our top speed of around 74 kph. Jason is an experienced cyclist and he couldn't control the bike. Fortunately, we had taken our old London frame, so at the last minute we shifted everything back to that. It is always best to go back to that which is safe and reliable. In the meantime, Daryl will no doubt keep working to make a tandem that is stiffer, without compromising on safety and performance.

It took time to acclimatise to Mexico. I found it difficult to breathe, sometimes even when standing still. For the first few days we took it easy. I roomed with Jason (Niblett) in a luxurious five-star hotel. We were warned not to drink the local water or eat red meat. Apparently, the meat had high levels of testosterone in it, which could affect urine sample outcomes. There was plenty of bottled water supplied and lots of tasty food.

We went to the Aguascalientes Bicentenary Velodrome to check the track, which looked good, but the velodrome had a vinyl roof held up by compressed air. To keep the air in and the roof up, all doorways were revolving and we had to move through a series of 'locks' – the door behind had to be closed, before you could open the next door and move forward. It felt like you were inside a gigantic balloon. It was impressive but had its problems too. When it got hot it smelled of plastic, and the interior temperatures changed as quickly and as dramatically as the weather outside. At our first training session in the morning it was bitterly cold. We rugged up with arm-warmers, jackets and gloves; anything to try to stay warm. On race day in the afternoon, it was 45° and stifling. I don't like hot weather anyway, but nobody enjoyed racing in this. I would soak my shirt under a tap and then wear it wet to stay cool. The oppressive heat made it more difficult to focus and recover.

Jason and I were not surprised to discover that Neil Fachie, the Scottish rider, had a new pilot, Pete Mitchell, for the sprint and kilometre events.

Mitchell, born in 1990, had sprung to prominence in 2007, winning the junior national title in the team sprint before achieving numerous podium finishes at national and European level in the sprint and team sprint. In 2009, he was named in the Team Sky+ HD track cycling team alongside names such as Chris Hoy and Victoria Pendleton.

Our first event was the Kilo, the event for which we were not initially selected, and we didn't get off to a good start. The tandem is held in a gate at the start. As I am sitting there waiting, I begin to zone in. I go over the event and 'see' the line we need to take. I am ready to get out of the saddle and be as explosive as I can. The start is vital, it's where you can create a great time and win – or lose – the Kilo time trial. I heard the beeps and suddenly realised I didn't know what number we were up to. Were we ten seconds from the start? Six seconds? Flustered and nervous I tried to see the counter, but it was out of range. I didn't have time to ask anyone and Jason was in his own zone. The beeps kept coming and all I could do was sit there and try to react as quickly as possible when Jason got up on his pedals. When he did I didn't do too badly, but it wasn't perfect and I reckon we lost half a second. I was so frustrated with myself.

However, they did well, as described in this email sent to me:

> The race day for the Kilo meant we were first off the rank. The temperature inside the track was 45 degrees. Some of the countries were warming up under the track because it was cooler there. We have new speed suits to wear, which means I need help to get it on. Dozens of fans were in the pits area but that didn't help, it just blew hot air around. Our warm up was good, but we missed the countdown on the starting line because no one had told me whether it started at 30 or 20 seconds. It was a good ride and we broke the world record. That would have won it if the British didn't beat us. They did a 59.4 to our 1:00.8. Because of the altitude, it took a long time to recover. We rode a 116" gear, very big. Resting up now for the sprint.

For a short time it looked like gold, until we were pipped by the British team. Australia's Paul Kennedy and Thomas Clarke (pilot) took the bronze after posting 1:2.640.

In the tandem sprint events, Jason and I again broke the world record in the flying 200 m qualifying, after posting 9.877 secs. However, in a mirror of the time trial event from the second day of competition, our time was pipped by Neil Fachie and Peter Mitchell when creating a new world record mark of 9.711. The British pair then took gold over us in the final in two straight heats. It turned out to be a tough day. In the Kilo we had pushed ourselves to the limit. There was only one day's rest before the sprints and there was some illness in the team. I was suffering from an upset stomach and breathlessness and we put this down to the altitude. Our sprint races were again held in seriously hot temperatures, seven gruelling races in one day. After the qualifying fly, we beat Denmark and Spain in straight sets, but I was very tired when we came up against the Brits. I am not getting any younger and for the sprints you need to recover quickly and be able to switch on and off mentally. Maybe we raced too hard in the qualifying events. We won by good margins in both and probably could have eased back to save our energy, but that's always tricky if you don't know your opposition. The Spanish had incredible acceleration, but were down a little on us in top-end speed. The Brits had both good acceleration and speed, but I felt we were in striking distance. They won by only half a bike length. I knew we had had a fair chance in Glasgow. I wanted to spend more time in the gym getting stronger, and I wanted a higher cadence. It's worth remembering that for the Brits, this is their job. They are professional – they get paid to cycle – and are probably on the track four or five times a week.

Back at home, Makala was happy with Kieran's silver. Kerry sent this email to the family:

> Hi there, just got Kieran's last email before his long journey home. He had a very successful championship, winning silver

> in the 1 km time trial and a silver in the sprint, also holding the second fastest qualifying time. The British team won gold in both, but they look pretty close. I think he has had a bit of altitude sickness, as have many, and it's been over 40 degrees in the velodrome every day, quite a challenge. Makala is rapt as she always wanted him to win a silver medal so that he has a set! We are all so looking forward to him coming home. We all hate this part of his cycling!
>
> Lots of love Kerry, Holly, Makala and Janae xxoo

Jason and I had broken world records in the heat of the Aguascalientes Velodrome while suffering from altitude sickness, and we now knew where our Glasgow competition was most likely to come from.

Team Australia had finished as the most successful country with 17 medals, including five rainbow jerseys. The rainbow jersey is the distinctive jersey worn by the reigning world champion in a bicycle racing discipline.

The team spirit was good with everyone supporting each other. It helped that we had enjoyed success, but our coach, Peter Day, is very enthusiastic and the athletes respect and are happy to work for him. Usually I like to get out and look around the places we visit. However in Mexico I just didn't feel safe. The drive to the velodrome in the minibus was scary. The roads were poor and if there were speed signs, nobody seemed to obey them. Even in the shopping centre we noticed guards walking around with submachine guns. The Mexican food was great and, for once, I was quite happy to stay in our hotel.

Our physiotherapist talked to the other teams about the altitude sickness and other medical issues. The teams that had an advantage were those that had been in Mexico longer than us, and some teams had done altitude training before they came.

* * *

Time does not stand still. As I was concentrating on the track Kilo and sprint for Glasgow, my crown as king of the track 4000 m pursuit event was taken by two much younger challengers.

Mick Curran (pilot, born in 1983) and Matt Formston (legally blind stoker born in 1978) had marketed themselves as 'Oz Tandem'. They got together in April 2012 and after only six weeks won their first Australian road championship. The boys lived in Wamberal on the Central Coast of New South Wales, and were great mates off the bike, enjoying surfing, rugby and working together in their business. Champion Vision is a coaching and consulting business that specialises in keynote presentations, motivational speaking and collaborative workshop delivery. Since forming, Oz Tandem had been dominant in Australian road para-cycling. They became Australian champions for the tandem road race and tandem road time trial in 2012 and defended both titles in 2013. They also won a 2013 World Cup gold medal in the road race in Matane, Canada, where they finished over 30 seconds in front of second place. They moved indoors to race in velodromes and their success continued. In 2014 in Mexico at altitude, they became the world champions and world record holders for the tandem 4000 m individual pursuit – Kieran's speciality.

Oz Tandem, 11 other tandem pairs and I set off to compete at the national para-road championships held in Echuca, Victoria, over the weekend of 10 and 11 May 2014. This event wasn't a part of my preparation program for Glasgow, but I went to promote the Clipsal Tandem Team project and to help a new pilot, 23-year-old Dave Parsons, be noticed by national selectors.

It turned out to be a rainy and foggy weekend and on Saturday all seemed to be going to script when Oz Tandem blitzed the 31.8 km time trial with a time of 42:08.69, and an average speed of 45.27 kph. Dave Parsons and Kieran rode into fourth place with a time of 45:06.87 (average: 42.29 kph) and good friend Mike Hoile, piloting Damien Williams, claimed fifth in 45:48.60 (average: 41.65 kph). It was another dominant display and title to Matt Formston and Mick Curran, and most expected a similar result in the longer road race set down to begin at 8 am the following day.

Although these championships are named as being held in Echuca, an Aboriginal name meaning 'meeting of the waters', situated close to the junction of the Goulburn, Campaspe and Murray rivers, the championship road track began approximately 60 km away in Rushworth. Here the male para-cyclists rode five laps of a relatively flat (maximum elevation of 172 m) 21.26 km course, a total of 106 km.

Mike Hoile and I enjoy time together reliving these longer road races. The times for the events are immaterial; what matters is the result and the margins between competitors. Tactics and strategy become critical factors, and so is communication and teamwork.

Mike uses heart monitors:

> Riding with Kieran is very different to riding with Damien. I need to tell Damien everything, whereas Kieran has a good idea of what is going on around him. Both Damien and I wear heart monitors and I have the heart readouts on my front handlebar. I know our optimum heart rates and race accordingly. We both use a number from 1 to 10 to communicate effort and to try to share the load evenly. A 10 is flat out, but a 10 at the start of the race is a lot different to a 10 at the finish. The effort you put in is often hard to gauge and comes with practice and familiarity. Some riders bring on their power smoothly and it's difficult to notice changes through the pedals. The tandem might be

> coasting along beautifully and suddenly you are aware that your partner's head is wobbling because they are doing most of the work.

On this Sunday, the race to be the 2014 National road champions was not going to be a one-sided affair. It turned into a classic race.

I had been dissatisfied with the 2013 road race at the same venue, especially the race tactics of Oz Tandem. They had stayed in the pack/peloton for the first three laps of the course and refused to do any of the work out front. They rested and then suddenly sprinted and broke away to win. I decided that this year we would stay with them and try to get them to work a bit harder. We were so focused on them that we didn't notice that Mike and Damien had broken away.

Mike's stoker, Damien, likes to sprint. As soon as the race begins, Damien wants to lead – a 106 km sprint would suit him perfectly! With 'Damo' urging him on, Mike found that they were out alone and leading:

> It was an accidental break away really. At the 15 km mark Damien and I were out near the front and riding up one of the hills. When I looked back I was surprised to find a gap between us and the pack. We crested the hill and decided to ride at 6s and 7s at about 42 kph and see what happened. We were surprised that the peloton didn't catch up for another 50 km.

Along with most of the peloton, Dave and I didn't know how far out in front Mike and Damien were, however we were more than happy with this situation. We stayed back with Oz Tandem and got them to take their turn on the front. They made about six small breaks and each time we were on their wheel. We tried to slow the pack down again, so we could be fresh for the sprint to the line. We eventually caught up to Mike and these small accelerated breaks continued. Each time Mike and Damien would drop off the back. When we slowed, they would tack on. It became a race in three.

Mike and Damien didn't have much left. But Mike decided to give it one more kick:

> Going up a hill early in the last lap Damien and I managed to pass the other two leading bikes. Both Oz Tandem and Kieran and Dave were out of their saddles, but Damien and I stayed seated. As we passed Oz Tandem, Damien, who is totally blind, said quite innocently and far too loudly, 'Why are we going so slow?' I think that from then on Oz Tandem thought we were fresher and their biggest danger. They watched our every move.

That was a mistake. Dave and I waited patiently. Oz Tandem cruised up on Mike's wheel until they were about 400 metres from the finish line, then clicked back their gears and took off. They flew past Mike and Damo. We paused, then kicked, and flew past both teams at 61 kph. Momentarily shocked, Oz Tandem recovered quickly. When I could see the line, it was a long way off, and Oz Tandem were gaining. Our recent sprint training came into play. It was a classic finish and after 106 km, we won by half a bike length!

Many of the stokers had been born visually impaired, but Mike Hoile's stoker, Damien 'Damo' Williams, is an especially courageous and resilient character. At 13 his left eye had to be removed after an accident while using a pair of pliers. To protect the remaining eye, he began wearing protective glasses (guaranteed by the manufacturer to be able to withstand the force of nearly any missile) and became an A-grade golfer. At age 27, while standing on the 18th hole of the Sanctuary Cove golf course and after putting his glasses up on to his head, an errant golf ball took out Damien's right eye. Damien and Mike have every reason to be very proud of their bronze medal.

Kieran and Mike laugh over some very close brushes with disaster. Mike has not so fond memories of one of Kieran's latest toys – a GPS navigation device:

> As part of the Tour Down Under we were invited to be part of a community ride starting in Woodside in the Adelaide Hills. We were flattered that a bus had been organised to pick us up, but not so happy that this was scheduled at 4 am. Kieran had just bought a GPS navigation device and was sure that by using this, we could leave a bit later than 4 am, ride to Woodside, and be there for the start. It was dark, our lights were ordinary and Kieran sat on the back of the bike telling me which roads to take. The GPS was clearly taking us there by the shortest (and craziest) route and I was getting quite used to instructions like 'right-left-right chicane' (we can do this quickly with care), 'left-hand elbow' (slow up) and 'right-hand sweeper' (flat out). As we were barrelling down another steep hill, from the back came a sudden 'T junction!' I knew we couldn't pull up in time. Thankfully Kieran had got it slightly wrong – it was a Y junction! I went right, we hit the gravel and somehow managed to keep the bike up. We walked back to look at our other option. The left lane went downhill with a very, very steep drop on the left side. Even mountain bikes wouldn't have saved us if we'd taken that route.

Every Thursday, Mike and I somehow crawl out of our warm beds to keep up a ritual. I leave home at 4.30 am and ride to Mike's. If he is not up (often) I'll tap on the window. Mike works long and late hours, so he likes his bed. We have a set circuit, which goes close to my home in Hallett Cove and returns through Glenelg. We can't use the bike tracks because we travel too quickly, so we run at race pace along bike lanes, usually in very light traffic.

Mike and I have pioneered tandems. It's taken a while for the solo bike riders to include the tandems. Cycling can be a bit cliquey and because Mike and I were pretty much the only ones on a tandem, the single cyclists didn't quite know how to relate to us.

And there's always the coffee and meticulously shaved legs. Why do cyclists shave their legs? Well, it's probably because we all do it. It's kind of a uniform. You often see male cyclists with facial hair, beards and hairy arms – but hairless legs. I guess there are aerodynamic advantages, but for me hair makes massage more painful, and cuts and abrasions heal quicker without hair. Our coffee drinking habit has also become a cyclist thing to do. It's a great way to catch up and have a chat with people ... but don't drink coffee before a long race!

Mike and I were in a coffee shop on a Saturday group ride day and analysing our latest ride. Australian professional road racing cyclist Victoria Veitch was at a table nearby listening to the conversation and aware of the energy and excitement as we analysed the ride, step by step. Curious she asked how she could get to ride a tandem. So the three of us came up with the concept of the Tandem Project. Victoria has progressed to be the team manager and driving force.

At a fundraiser in the Mercedes-Benz showrooms in Adelaide, Victoria stressed that the program is not just a way to provide vision-impaired people with a 'recreational experience':

> The purpose of the program is to produce road competent tandem riders, with each program running for ten to 12 weeks duration for basic level graduation. A further six to nine months of advanced training is offered for athletes who have been offered a position within the racing team. The Program

> Scholarship Scheme is designed to attract funding both to the Project itself, and to individual athletes. The scholarships are all administered through the team, to ensure contributions are put to the best use in supporting the athletes towards their competition ambitions.

Victoria is a neuro-physiotherapist and the group that she works for (Edwina Reid Neuro Physiotherapy Services in Rose Park) and Mike's cleaning company (Ozone Cleaning Specialists) are sponsors of the Tandem Project, along with a couple of other businesses. The search for sustainable support for this key service is ongoing.

Mike and his wife Jill (who provide a home not only for all equipment, but also for many riders who need a bed so they can be up before the sun rises for an early workout), team manager Victoria and I (as group mentor) all work voluntarily. We think one of the reasons the Project is growing so effectively is because we all ride tandems – and with great enthusiasm.

In 2014, Beau Wootton was 15 years old and a skilful vision-impaired cyclist in the Tandem Project team. Like Kieran, Beau had optic atrophy and, also like Kieran, his enthusiasm was contagious, as was his competitiveness. Although Beau was suffering from seizures and other health issues, his health specialists and Victoria Veitch encouraged him to keep riding. Beau is one of the many people touched by Kieran. In a tribute, Beau wrote:

> I was introduced to cycling by my teacher, mentor, friend and hero Kieran Modra. His words and encouragement have kept me going when I just wanted to give up on everything! The most important words that resonate with me are 'be your very best, be humble, be honest – and love what you do'. I would like to thank all the wonderful pilots who enrich my life. Without

> you, cycling would only be a pipe dream. I would love to follow in Kieran's footsteps and one day represent Australia in cycling.

Victoria, Mike and I have established the most successful template in Australia to enable competition standard vision-impaired riders to ride on the road. We all believe that the only thing worse than being blind is someone who has sight, but no vision.

The Tandem Project has flourished and now there are half a dozen of our bikes regularly being ridden around Adelaide. Cyclists are often fascinated by the power of these bikes and we are attracting pilots who want to try something different and help our growing VI cohort.

There is still danger involved. Recently, when riding city bound up Anzac Highway, a driver travelling in the opposite direction crossed the median strip and continued to drive head on at the squad in the bike lane. Apparently, he wanted to turn into a street (as he later attempted to explain to the police) and didn't see the problem in travelling into oncoming traffic the final 50 metres to get there. All the tandems did a brilliant job in taking evasive action to get out of the way of the vehicle; however, one of the single bike squad members was cleaned up in the carnage and hit the road at 48 kph.

Uncle Andy: *You gave an inspiring speech at The Tandem Project fundraising evening, Kieran. Do you enjoy public speaking?*

Kieran: Well I was kind of forced into public speaking because of what I'd done. Sport brought all my issues to the fore. That became me; that's what people were interested in; it made me different from everybody else. It was scary in the beginning, but when I believed people were genuinely interested, I grew in confidence. It is what I can do despite my lack of sight that interests people, so I think about it a lot. When I'm speaking to an audience, I treat it like a conversation, as if I'm just talking to someone else. Of course, I like to know what sort of audience is in front of me and I usually joke that I won't be able to tell if they all fall asleep during the talk.

But your message is so positive ...

Well there's not a lot of point in grizzling or grumping. The reality is that I can't see like most people. Does that limit me? Well, yes. Does that stop me from trying? No. The more you reinforce the positive things, the more you start believing them. Public speaking takes lots of energy, but I am speaking about things I am passionate about and it's very rewarding.

I think that you fool people because you don't look blind. When I'm talking to you, your face and eyes move naturally.

I've learned all of that. I would really like to know the face I'm looking at, but then I would need to stare, or move into personal space. So I have to sacrifice that curiosity, or look at photos. It can become a problem when people expect me to know them. I've become pretty good at listening to and recognising voices. I still often try to hide my blindness. I've got a lot of friends who still don't know that I'm so blind.

It's hard to believe that you could be in any situation where you might be embarrassed or overwhelmed.

Well this is nothing to do with cycling, but I can think of two situations I find embarrassing. The first relates to finding the person I'm after. Usually when I'm in a school, I'm mentoring a student with a disability. First, I need to find their room, and then it gets worse because I can't peer closely into all the faces in there to find the right person. Teachers help me avoid this embarrassment. At parties or in large groups of people, I will have difficulty finding Kerry if I leave the group for any reason. Kerry is good because she will wave to me when I return, but the kids don't like her doing this.

And the other situation?

Would you believe that another embarrassing situation involves food. I find buffets or smorgasbords difficult because I can't see the food properly. Clearly, I can't go up and closely peer at each foodstuff. It not only looks silly, but it's not hygienic. Sometimes I just guess, but generally it's Kerry to the rescue. She will get me a nice big plate of all the things I like.

Oh, and on the food served at buffets, the trickiest thing for me is the sandwiches cut into triangles. I can't see where one sandwich starts and another one ends. So, if I try to take one, I generally get the middle parts and the stuff inside goes everywhere!

I think that's happened to most of us!

12 Glasgow and the Power Monkey

2014

I was nervously excited about representing Australia at the 2014 Glasgow Commonwealth Games. Not only was I exploring another overseas destination, but I was also taking on sprint cycling, a specialty that didn't necessarily suit my physical capabilities, and presented huge challenges. I was looking forward to mixing with able-bodied athletes, many of whom were my sporting heroes.

It promised to be the pinnacle of my sporting career. However, at age 42 and father of three daughters, I knew in my heart that our preparation was compromised. I felt like we weren't doing enough training right from the word go. Jason is a raw sprinter with very good acceleration and as a Commonwealth Games team sprinter, he was used to one lap. I knew that with tandems we required a bigger base of endurance, especially for our longest race of four laps. I wanted to do more, but in the back of my mind was the knowledge that I was nearing my last race, and I faced a fear of crashing. Sprinting is scary and we had a lot of mechanical breakages. The tandem flexes enormously and when I crash now, I usually break bones. The advantage of this lighter training load was that I had more days at home and Kerry was happier with this, but I knew we should have done more in Australia.

When the Australian cycling team arrived in Newport, Wales, for our pre-Games camp, Jason and I ramped up our training. I really enjoyed working with the able-bodied Commonwealth

Games riders too. I was particularly impressed and inspired by another South Australian, Jack Bobridge, and enjoyed both observing and then chatting with him. There was no discrimination between those in the Paralympic team and those who were able-bodied. All were accepted as equals.

Glasgow was now only a bus trip away and I was impatient to find out what the atmosphere was like in the Commonwealth Games Village. I had assumed that with the higher level of sporting achievement attained by more able-bodied athletes, there would be higher levels of enthusiasm and a more vibrant atmosphere within the Village. I had often asked officials and voluntary helpers at the Paralympics which they preferred – the Olympics or Paralympics. Their responses had surprised me, because almost all stated a preference for the latter.

The Games ran very well, just like London ... but the electricity and atmosphere weren't there. The other athletes were friendly and approachable, but the aura of the Paralympics was missing. I spent a lot of time trying to work out why. In Glasgow the people moved around with athletic ease, but at the Paralympics you see it all – the amputees, wheelchairs, and crutches, those whose burdens are easily identified. Here are people proud of their achievements and they stand tall. They bring energy and excitement and you can't help but marvel at their spirit and be inspired by their stories.

Among these able-bodied athletes and accompanied by my very popular pilot, Jason Niblett, I felt the recurring presence of an old habit. I was immersed in a predominantly able-bodied atmosphere and at first I felt able-bodied too. It was a unique feeling. However, as I looked around and saw the high-profile athletes, I became aware of my disability and once again, like a boy at school, I tried to hide it.

I have fond memories of my Glasgow experience. I enjoyed the set-up of the Village, although along with Jason I found it difficult to find any privacy – or sleep. We slept in the lounge room of one of the units, converted temporarily into a bedroom for the Games. The walls were paper-thin and one could hear clearly any conversations going on in nearby rooms.

And once again we had mechanical issues. We are both thickset, big-muscled athletes and our combined massive force through the pedals creates an enormous strain on the bike. We had problems with the chain flicking over the rear cog, because the frame flexes so much. This made a loud crunching noise. Combating that problem by pulling the chain drum tight wasn't efficient, but it was the only way the bike could cope with our combined three to four thousand watts of power put down on the pedals, especially at the standing start.

Our World Championship nemesis, Neil Fachie, had nicknamed himself 'Power Monkey' and been re-united with Scottish pilot Craig MacLean.

Craig MacLean MBE has a long list of cycling achievements at Olympic, Commonwealth and UCI levels. He represented Great Britain and Northern Ireland at the 2000 Summer Olympics in Sydney and the 2004 Summer Olympics in Athens, winning a silver medal in the team sprint with Sir Christopher Hoy at the 2000 Olympics. Craig also won a bronze medal for Scotland in the team sprint at the 2002 Commonwealth Games, followed by a gold medal in the event at the 2006 Commonwealth Games in Australia. As well, MacLean had won medals in five UCI Track World Championships in the team sprint from 1999 to 2004.

MacLean had returned to the sport in its Paralympic form as a sighted guide and piloted Neil Fachie to two gold medals at the 2011

UCI Para-cycling Track World Championships in the tandem B sprint and tandem B 1000 m time trial. He had also piloted Anthony Kappes to a gold medal in the 2012 Paralympic Games.

Along with Sir Christopher Hoy, MacLean is widely accepted as a key figure in the rise of British track cycling. In Glasgow, he would be a formidable foe.

We were enjoying the racing – and so were the crowds packed inside the velodrome. There was a tremendous interest in the tandems because they were unusual and different. The crowds were off their seats when we raced. The noise following us around the track was exhilarating and uplifting.

In the Kilo, we set an outstanding time of 1:02.244, two seconds faster than any other team. With the full weight of the predominantly Scottish crowd behind them, Fachie and MacLean beat our time by a mere .148 of a second to claim the gold medal.

I can only describe this race as a 'mad minute'. It is over in a flash. After 40 seconds your legs turn to jelly as the lactic acid builds up and you can feel a loss of bike speed, but you just push on. The wind is blowing through your hair, the crowd is cheering and you try to focus on keeping the upper body still, but despite all the training, your body is straining to get every bit of energy on to the pedals.

We were disappointed to lose, but now focused on our next chance to beat the Scottish champions. We were amazed at how quickly they began but then they faded quite dramatically over the kilometre. Losing by so little did give us heart for the sprints.

Sprints day began very well for us. In the qualification session, Jason and I set a new world record in the flying 200 m and were seeded first. The Scottish duo was seeded second, giving us a clear psychological advantage, and in the best of three, we won the first heat convincingly.

On 27 September 2014, Neil Fachie was to tweet in MailOnline:

> The morning session was such a struggle for us; we were just so fatigued from yesterday. Qualifying didn't go that well and I felt awful after it. We got through the semi-final and it was a real effort. The Aussies were flying. They killed us in qualifying and I knew they had a lot they could use against us. They are such a talented team and I knew it was going to be a struggle. The first ride proved that!

The second heat turned out to be a thriller. We got to the front and wound up for home and the gold. We had won the first race quite comfortably, but we figured that they had a smaller gear on and they changed that for the second heat. In the second heat we led out and wound up to go as quickly as we could. I thought we had it! This was it ... this was it! Then I could see them coming around on my hip with 50 metres to go. No, I thought, no! They began to pass. I wanted to reach out and pull them backwards. I could see the gold medal slipping away. We had put everything into it and I knew when we walked off that track that I didn't have anything left in my legs. To make matters worse, they didn't give Jason and me enough time to recover, which affected both of us. We hadn't done enough back-end training, so we didn't have the stamina base.

When Jason and I lined up for the final heat, we hadn't told each other how worn out we felt. We gave it everything we had and it came down to who had the better legs. The Scots came over us convincingly and won the gold. I was probably down 50% in power for that final heat. The Scots were tired too, but able to sustain their strength for longer, and we both applauded their effort.

A gold medal is the ultimate way to substantiate excellence in preparation and performance. You strive for first place and the gold medal and I think our frustration was heightened by the fact that we were so close, so incredibly close. When you win silver the questions start. Then you begin to look for answers. What could we have done differently?

Both pilots raced well tactically. It was good racing. I am proud of our effort. For me to shift across from track endurance racing to sprinting and to come a close second to the best sprint tandem team in the world for a long time is an achievement. It's hard for me; I've been used to winning gold for such a long time and it's brought me back a peg. It's made me more aware of striving for excellence, rather than expecting it. Winning makes post-ride evaluation easy. Coming second gets you thinking and re-evaluating; it's something I haven't had to do for a long time. In a way it is energising, because I realise there is passion still there. It was important for me to get the silvers – but I could have got at least one gold!

Interviewed for the ABC sports radio program 'Grandstand' immediately after the final race, Kieran said:

> Ultimately it was who had the most in their legs for the third race. Jason did a fantastic job. He was a brilliant tactician and I commend him. I come from a pursuit background and Neil's is sprinting, so I'm stepping into his event on his home track. We were big rivals for them and they weren't going to just hand it over. We fought for it as much as we could. I commend them too. They did a brilliant job. I even enjoyed racing them because they really showed some world class.

The racing was absorbing and had the stands rollicking, especially as the local hero turned a 0–1 deficit into a 2–1 win. Jason was also magnanimous in the face of disappointment:

> Craig (MacLean) and I have raced each other before; at Olympic level he has a superb record. The Glasgow crowd was treated to all-time best tandem racing. It's a shame that the tandems aren't at the Rio Olympics – it could have been a real spectacle. We didn't get the gold medals around our necks, but our world record in the flying 200 this morning and the atmosphere in here still makes it very special. The British have dominated this event. I think they appreciated us putting on a good show; it really promotes para-tandem cycling. Only good will come of this.

Neil Fachie, now a Scottish hero, said to the press:

> I've been lucky to be on top of the podium a few times, but this is the first time I've raced for Scotland. It was hard not to get teary-eyed when we got our medals. You don't really consider yourself inspirational, but it is nice when people come up to you with compliments. There are so many people with visual impairments in Scotland and the UK, and the sad thing is we only have two British bikes here and there is not even an English tandem team. There are so many people who could be taking up the opportunity and if anyone is inspired by me to do that, then I am happy.

A justifiably proud Kerry emailed Marlene and me on a Rhine-Danube river cruise:

> It was a fantastic showcase of tandem racing and we are so proud that Kieran was there to represent Australia and show off the sport and his talent to the world. Feeling relieved that the racing is over and he now has time to enjoy what the rest of the Games offer.

* * *

I now faced a very important decision. Was Glasgow to be my final international tandem experience? I tried to create a mindset where there was no cycling or national or international competition. I had so many questions. What would life be like after sport? I am fully aware that mine is a very selfish sport. Was I jeopardising relationships with my family? With the increased danger in sprinting, how many crashes could my body take? Could I rely on the equipment we were using? Why did we have so many tyre blowouts and mechanical failures?

Many people are fascinated by what I'm doing and where I'm going. What would happen when I could no longer talk about this? Who I am is so interlinked with sport. For the most part I've enjoyed being in the limelight and I've probably enjoyed the respect of my peers and protégés because I could still 'walk the talk'. Would I still have their respect if I stopped?

I love food! My training burns up calories and so I can pretty much eat anything and not put on excess weight. I always put on weight (not the muscle kind) in my 'rest year' after the Games. Would I turn into a beach ball?

And the travel? How much would I miss jetting around the world to see wonderful scenery and meet inspirational people?

A portion of our income comes from Australian Government support in sport and once I retire I would need to find work. I have become accustomed to an athlete's life; the flexibility with work hours and workdays. Could I even find work, work that would suit my lifestyle and disability? Could I handle nine to five, five days a week?

Then I thought about the positives. No more blood samples for testing drugs. No more needles! No more waiting in queues of athletes hopping up and down on the spot waiting for their turn to pee into a jar in front of an official! No more massages. I have a lot of muscle bulk and they get their fingers in deep to knead out the tightness. They are experts at finding the very sore bits and squeezing them. They say that you will be sore for a while, and when you come back sore the next day they rip into you again. My pain threshold is reasonably high, but these people sure know how to bring it down! No more hard, painful training sessions.

I couldn't see myself going on to Rio. I knew they were conspiring to try to get me there. I decided that I had enjoyed what I had achieved. I was not sure I had the passion now anyway. It certainly didn't come as naturally to me as it did ten years ago. I wanted to keep my memories as fond memories, rather than becoming redundant and old news. I didn't seem to have that 'dagger-eyed' sort of competitive spirit that most of my opponents had. I enjoyed seeing other people succeed. It was good to see the Scots on the podium. I've had so much attention for a long time and it was nice to see the cameras focused on them. Sometimes it's nice to sit back.

I retired.

13 Retirement and the C word

2015

After Glasgow and now 'retired', I slipped into a lifestyle without the pressure of cycling competition. Kerry and I set about to reclaim some of the family time lost to my former stricter training regimes and travel.

Holly, Makala and Janae were now all attending the same local school and I was able to spend more time with them. Gone were the difficulties of being involved with and travelling to different schools, most often located some distance away. However the girls continued to struggle. They expended so much energy, and every so often a minority of peers would tease them and shake their confidence. They had enough friends to support them if they opened up, but they didn't realise this.

It's more difficult for them than for me. It might be their personalities, or that they are girls. We are trying to make home life a haven. We encourage them to have friends over but the problem is that they want to come home to relax. When they are with others they feel they must put on a brave face, when in reality they might be hurting inside. And it takes a lot of effort to be brave.

The girls are getting some support at their school, but support is not the issue. The issue is making them confident enough to ask for help. The two battles are getting the support and then getting them to accept it.

I am aware of the pressure on Kerry and the toll this takes. We are trying to create a positive environment at home to combat all the negativity the kids have in their lives, but it puts a lot of stress on Kerry. Being the caring mum that she is, the children generally unload the frustrations of the school day on her when they come home. She takes the weight of their problems on her shoulders and tends to bottle it all up. She really struggles and my role is to support her, so that she can offload that stuff. We spend a lot of time talking.

I am in a unique position because I share a disability with Holly and Makala. Yet I need care as well and that adds to the pressure on Kerry.

Kerry sees both sides:

> I can see our children growing through their problems. What Kieran has had to face, and how he has overcome that, gives them hope for the future. But they are all individuals and are learning to cope. Kieran has done this through sport. The girls will need to find their own ways.

An active social networker, Kerry wrote on her Facebook page:

> Isn't it interesting how people who have been educated on a topic think they know more than a person who is actually living it? My girls inspire me every day. They get up and face the day knowing that some of the day will be challenging, their feelings may be hurt, they will have to explain why they do things differently than others, they will be put in a position that is uncomfortable for them. But they still come home, smile, laugh about the things that were uncomfortable and sometimes cry about them. But they always get up the next day and face those challenges again. We could all learn so much from these young people if we all stopped and took the time to listen.

Kerry feels that people think she wants Kieran to spend more time at home and that she resents the enormous time that he spends on his sport. In an impassioned email to me, she wrote:

Hi Andy,

I sometimes feel that people think I'm not supportive, that I'm resentful for the time he spends away. Life gets so busy. The girls have everyday issues coping with their vision impairment. I'm forever at school trying to get them the help they need and forever telling the girls how great they are and how successful they will be, what great people they are, that their disability doesn't have to define them – constantly reassuring them that they will be okay. I guess Kieran's cycling takes him away from all of this. So I often feel like they are my constant battles, and I must battle through on my own. To be honest it can be exhausting. Sometimes I wish this was something we battled through together. Now that Kieran is spending time home after retiring from the Commonwealth Games he can see a little more of what is going on with the girls; it's becoming something we, for the first time, battle together. And it's a relief not to be doing it on my own, almost like a weight has been lifted. I know how dedicated Kieran must be to be the best he can and I want him to succeed in everything he does. I know how happy he is and how much being good at this means to him and I will always be his biggest supporter and try and keep things together at home. But what life has dealt our family has caught up with me and some days are a real battle to get through. There is a real feeling of losing myself in all that has happened.

And honestly there are times I have felt resentful. I know at times Kieran felt I wasn't supportive but I guess I often felt the same. Watching the girls' everyday struggles has broken my heart. I sometimes feel that there is nothing left for anyone else.

Because Kieran had lost his part-time job mentoring and helping VI students at a secondary school, both parents could see the girls off in the morning and be there to welcome them home after school finished.

I sort of fell out of my mentoring job, just after Glasgow. When you work for the Department for Education and Child Development (DECD) there is so much paperwork. You have to reapply every year, and previously I'd had help with my enrolment forms from SASVI. People in the Department had even encouraged me to apply for permanency. I thought that I had everything in place, so I was surprised to find there seemed to be nothing happening. When I rang, they told me that the money for my job had been allocated elsewhere. It's probably my fault because I should have checked and re-checked that the forms were in place.

I've always enjoyed being there and working with the kids, but I was becoming increasingly frustrated because I feel that in modern society they are being packed in cotton wool. I took risks growing up and learnt from outcomes, but parents and teachers today are very protective. I tried to talk to teachers about this, but generally felt my words were falling on deaf ears. With 'duty of care' these days, no one is prepared to take risks and while I understood this, I felt frustrated by it. I enjoyed working there, but there was so much more I wanted to add to the quality of life and development of the students in my care. The VI students who were prepared to take risks caused problems at the school, because they were a potential danger to themselves and those around them. I think the school managed this well, and it's probably just where society is currently.

* * *

Kerry and I took on two projects to ease the growing family frustrations.

Firstly we tackled the problems associated with living with three growing children in a very small house. Makala and Janae had always shared a tiny bedroom, so it was time for some major extension work. The builders arrived just before I left for Glasgow, so Kerry and the girls bore the brunt of the initial inconveniences. However we were all very happy to add a main bedroom with ensuite, so that the two younger girls could have their own bedroom space and all share another living area. Kerry and I rendered the outside of the new extensions and did all the painting.

A few years earlier we had bought a campervan and now was the time to use it. We arranged a six-week caravanning holiday with Kerry's parents, already well-equipped and keen caravanners.

Setting out in April, Kerry remembers the excitement:

> This was our first real family holiday and we were all so excited. Holly was a little anxious about keeping her phone charged and about Wi-Fi availability! Luckily for us, Mum and Dad had travelled up through Queensland before, and this is where we were keen to go. Dad and I sat down with a map and planned a rough route. We wanted to take the girls to the theme parks on the Gold Coast, but we also wanted to show them outback Queensland. We took our camper trailer, and Mum and Dad had their caravan, soon to be named the 'Hyatt'. Compared to our camper, their van was complete luxury with a toilet, shower, washing machine, heating, cooling and microwave.
>
> We stayed in caravan parks and enjoyed great free camping. A couple of our favourite spots along the way were Lightning Ridge (opal country – my favourite!), Nindigully where we stayed at the pub and got to listen to my all-time favourite country music songs, and Boondooma, where we were rained in for two days. Of course, the Gold Coast was a highlight. It was an amazing holiday and we had so much fun. We lived

> as (Holly called it) 'hobos' for a few weeks. The girls said they enjoyed outback Queensland the most. We got to Bundaberg before we had to turn around and come home.

The girls like to go to the caravan parks because of the showers. I prefer the National Parks where we can be a little more isolated, be by ourselves and appreciate nature. But the girls are teenagers and love their phones and computers. They don't appreciate being too far away from an internet provider.

Caravan parks do provide challenges to the visually impaired. Kerry has a routine:

> Locating the campervan when the parks are busy is a problem. We all go to the toilets together after we park the van so the girls know where to go. They usually walk together around the park. Holly said that they are always thinking – thinking of explanations in case they pick the wrong van or toilets. We never had any problems when we were away this time. Holly said that you just take note of landmarks to make sure you always know where to go.

The family would like to do this again. Kerry knows how good it was for the girls:

> We thoroughly enjoyed it. It was one of the best experiences we've had as a family. I feel like it brought us all closer together. It was a great time for us all to relax and be together and a place for the girls to let their hair down and just be themselves. Their vision isn't a problem when it's just us and close family. They are themselves and that is special.

* * *

I continued to ride with Mike Hoile and the team in the Tandem Project, but with the lead up to Glasgow, I hadn't been able to be as actively involved as I would have liked. The Project grows as long as we can find stokers for the program. To get VIs on a bike is one thing, but to get them to push the boundaries outside of their comfort zone and excel is difficult. A lot of them have been mollycoddled in their younger lives. Kieran Murphy is one stoker who has come through to a higher level competition. Able-bodied tandems ride with the VIs and it helps to put able-bodied cyclists on the back of a tandem, so that they can experience what a stoker feels. The Tandem Project is predominantly road race focused, so I like to take part in road races, time trials and the Road Nationals regardless of my level of fitness at the time. It's a way of supporting other members of our TP squad by being a mentor, supporter and benchmark.

So I couldn't resist an invitation from Nathan Hunter to ride in the 2015 National para-cycling road race held at Trinity College's Gawler River Campus, 50 km north-east of Adelaide. The course was 87 km over five laps. Nathan Hunter was a promising pilot and we gave Oz Tandem a terrific race. The two tandems raced together and inevitably it came down to a sprint finish. After Glasgow I was better prepared for this and we had a good chance of winning until our bike chain came off and we had to roll over the line 10 seconds behind Matt Formston and Michael Curran. The third placegetters, Damien Williams and Mathew Miller, were nearly two minutes behind. Once again Oz Tandem had prevailed.

The Modra family are close and Kieran's branch is no different. Sister Tania married Simon Hill, who was completing a doctorate in mechanical engineering. After time in Belgium where Simon worked in universities and Tania worked as a business analyst at Toyota's European headquarters, they moved to Japan for Simon to continue post-doctoral work. With their son Caleb they returned to Sydney where their second son Jonathan was born and where Simon retrained as an Anglican minister at the Moore Theological College. The Modra and Hill families were happy when Tania and Simon took up a parish appointment in coastal Largs Bay near Adelaide, much closer to home after ten years away.

Brother Mark had continued to farm on the Eyre Peninsula. Winner of a Nuffield Research Scholarship in 2004, he married Tamara Neldner in 2010 and has three daughters and a son. Mark bought the Modra home farm in Yeelanna from his Uncle John in 2014.

Kieran's eldest brother, Darren, worked in Adelaide in computing. Widely acclaimed as a tech whiz, he married Tammy Wilson in 2003. Tammy works within the South Australian Government. The couple grew close to all, but especially to Kieran and Kerry's three girls.

In October Tammy and Darren had devastating news to tell the family. Medical tests had revealed that Darren had terminal cancer. There was no cure. In an email to the wider family, Tammy spoke openly about all that had happened with Darren; he didn't care who knew, he just didn't want to have to talk about it.

After various discussions with two specialists and their doctor, Darren chose to undertake chemo with an antibody. They were informed that with this treatment Darren could expect to live another two years. He began treatment immediately.

Kerry was one of the first people Tammy and Darren rang with the news. She remembers the phone call:

> We knew that Darren was having a colonoscopy. Tammy and Darren rang us and told us about the initial result, which at that stage was quite positive. When Tammy rang and told me of Darren's cancer spreading, Kieran was not home. I had to tell Kieran of Darren's cancer when he got home. That was

> one of the hardest things I have ever done. It was awful. We are so fortunate to have built up a close relationship with both Tammy and Darren. They have been, and still are, one of our biggest supports. It's heartbreaking to go through this and feel helpless to do anything to make it easier for them.

On hearing the news from Kerry, we immediately went to Darren and Tammy's home to comfort and support them. We didn't take our daughters or tell them the whole story when we returned home. We were coming to terms with the shock as well. Like Kerry, I didn't want to traumatise the girls. We tried to dampen it down a bit, because they get hung up on those sorts of things. We said that he was unwell and I think that for some time they thought along these lines. But then we talked about the seriousness of the situation to help them prepare for the inevitable shock. The girls were very close to Darren and it was difficult for them to deal with.

Kerry remembers:

> We sat them down and told them that Darren had cancer; that it had moved throughout his body and that the doctors had treatment options for him. At first we didn't tell the girls that it was terminal. We were hoping that treatment would give Darren more time, which would give us many more memories and many more laughs, which is what we all love to do together.
>
> The girls had a really special relationship with Darren. He had come to Father's Day events when Kieran had been away and also played many games on the Wii with them, which they had always loved. He had enjoyed many birthdays, roller-skating, laser tag and such fun times together. They phoned him for iPad and iPhone advice.
>
> The girls had seen physical changes in Darren since he started treatment. It's interesting that Holly asked lots of questions and struggled at school, trying not to think about

it. Makala openly voiced her worries and asked questions all the time. Janae was also concerned but had a different outlook, perhaps because of what she's been through (with her heart operations). I'd spent a lot of time talking about how amazing doctors were before her surgeries, and I think she believed that because they helped her they would be able to help Darren.

It's so hard to watch someone you love go through what Darren faced every day. We tried to look at the positive results, to spend as much time with them as we could and be there for them. We still laughed together and enjoyed each other's company.

I admired my brother and tried to ride to his place every week and get to his chemo sessions. Darren just sat in a chair while they fed drugs into him. He was a battler and stoic, just taking it quietly, but I imagine he felt frustrated and Tammy had to deal with that. I admired him, I was inspired by him and it drew us closer.

Darren continued to bravely receive treatment until all realised that it was not effective. Coming off treatment, he farewelled his former work colleagues and family and died peacefully at home with Tammy by his side on 28 December 2016. Tammy asked Kieran to speak on behalf of the family at Darren's funeral. As deeply devastated as we all were, he spoke as brightly as he could about the wonderful attributes of his brother and friend. Vale to a lovely, gentle man.

(At Kieran's parents' 50th – golden – wedding celebration in the Good Shepherd Lutheran Church Hall, Hallett Cove in November 2015.)

Kieran: I've been wanting to tell you this, but I'm a bit nervous. I'm back into training.

Uncle Andy: *Do you mean you are training for the Paralympics?*

Well ... yes. But they haven't found me a pilot yet.

But, Kieran, you promised Makala that you had retired from competitive cycling. She was delighted with your silver medals because it made up the complete set. Is she okay with this?

She seems pretty happy with my decision.

And what about Kerry? Doesn't she want you at home a little more?

I think she's happy that I've got something to do that keeps me fit. At least I'm out from under her feet ... and away from our pantry as well. After Glasgow, I spent time with the family and Kerry enjoyed that. We created a family unit again and so I'm getting a lot of support from Kerry and the kids. You sound a little shocked.

I am. I am completely blind-sided. It's kind of funny though.

Why?

Well of all the people who should have guessed this would happen, it should have been me. As the writer of your biography I have made it very clear to our readers that you do this time after time.

It's all happened a bit later this time though. I think I was a little burnt out after Glasgow. Also, I didn't get a break after London because it was straight into the sprints training. I've only got two months to the nationals and as yet I don't have a pilot – or a bike!

Did you approach Cycling Australia, or did they approach you?

I approached Peter Day, the Australian para-coach and told him I was keen to come back. He said that he would be happy if I did, but he wanted me to be sure and that the commitment this posed was okay with the family. Now they have to chase around for a pilot. This is not an easy process. We need to find someone who is qualified and very strong and, most important of all, motivated to take on the challenge of tandems.

Are you feeling fit?

I'm getting there.

What about Oz Tandem? Will they be there?

Yes ... as always.

You must beat them to progress?

Yes. They'll probably take only one Australian men's pursuit team to Rio, unless another team has enough points to justify taking two.

How many Paralympics would this be?

My eighth, which seems weird.

Why?

Well, when I started my participation in Seoul, fellow South Australian Libby Kosmala had already been to four Paralympics. I thought that was amazing, and she's been to all the Paralympics that I've attended as well. She is a legend, winning 13 medals, nine of them gold.

You're not going to try to beat her record, are you?

Well no, because I am going to retire, maybe after the next Games.

Retire again you mean ...

My first goal is to get on that plane to Rio – and that is not going to be easy.

14
Oh, did someone say the word 'Rio'?

2015–2016

Two months out from selection trials, management found a tandem pilot and flew him to Adelaide to meet me.

David Edwards had enjoyed an outstanding junior career. Born in Alice Springs in the Northern Territory in 1993, his family moved to northern Queensland. He only started cycling thanks to a gift from a cousin:

> I started cycling when I was 13. A cousin gave me a bike and I was ten kilometres out of town so I would ride to school. I started working with a local triathlon coach, and soon I was riding in Cairns and Townsville; Brisbane followed.

David was not only winning in his age category, but also breaking time trial records and winning criteriums and road races on a regular basis. He was quickly identified as a rare talent and was invited into the QAS High Performance Program as one of Australia's future stars of cycling.

In 2011 David finished third in the World U19 UCI World Time Trial Championships. He also had a string of notable domestic performances, including second in the U19 Oceania Time Trials and second in the National Selection road race.

In 2013 David was invited to join the famous French team AG2R La Mondiale (U23 team). David's results and potential were strong enough for his contract to be extended for the 2014 season:

> In 2013–14 I was living in France and riding with a French team in Division 1 of the French Cup. I medalled at the Junior Worlds in Copenhagen. I won a national title in Under 17s and was getting better and better, but then the improvement plateaued. When I finished high school in Atherton, I came to Brisbane to study Psychology and I've nearly finished that degree through correspondence with the University of New England. Cycling Australia approached me and asked me if I would be interested in being a pilot for Kieran Modra. Now this was kind of weird, because one of the recent discussion topics in my Psychology course in the area of sport and disabilities was on Kieran Modra. So when I was approached, and even though I'd never ridden a tandem before, I was captivated by the coincidence.

With only eight weeks to train together, David and I began our partnership by wobbling around the track. I was amazed at how quickly he improved and how hard he worked at technique and fitness.

The tandem events to be held at the national titles in Adelaide in December 2015 were shaping up to be the best in history with Kieran, David and Oz Tandem featuring in a superb field. Oz Tandem pilot Michael Curran was well aware of the importance of success when he told Cycling Australia:

> It is a massive showcase of Aussie tandems. The carrot of Rio has brought newcomers to the game, and also the 'who's who' back into the mix. Although we cannot spend our energy thinking about or guessing where the others are at, it still adds that extra element to each session knowing the other bikers will be bringing their A game. The healthy competition is only a good thing for Australian cycling. It brings the best out in everyone.

In a Newcastle-based NBN television interview, the interviewer commented: 'To achieve their goals they'll have to defeat a legend of the sport, a seven-time Paralympian …' Mick Curran added: 'Kieran Modra has appeared on the list again. That guy has retired three times and his name has popped up again. You just can't keep that guy away!'

Formston and Curran riding as Oz Tandem were looking to claim their third consecutive pursuit national title and would also line up to defend their kilometre time trial crown. Curran said:

> Expectations for the Kilo are somewhat relaxed, it's the pursuit we have been training for. We always set high expectations on ourselves heading into the Nationals and this year is no different. Simply put, without performing our best at these championships, there will be no Rio; that's how much of an important stepping stone they are in the grand goal of Rio.

Marlene and I drove to Adelaide to watch Kieran and David ride for the national pursuit title. It was hellishly hot inside Adelaide's velodrome (The Super Drome) on 17 December. Bushfires and dust storms had just ravaged the countryside north of the venue and Adelaide was in the middle of breaking meteorological records for the longest number of consecutive 40-degree days in December.

Kieran came to greet us in his normal enthusiastic and upbeat manner. No, it wasn't hot enough, he told me. Cyclists liked it like this because the heat swelled the track boards, making for a firmer, smoother and therefore faster surface. The air would be thinner and that meant faster times. No, he wasn't nervous. A bit unsure, but he and his tandem pilot had taken it easy on the previous evening's Kilo event to concentrate on today's favourite, the pursuit. He sat down and quietly texted Kerry.

Sister Tania turned up and we positioned ourselves near the start/finish line, with occasional visits to an area under the members' air-conditioned bar. Someone up there had graciously left a window ajar and the cool air drifted down to us below.

The heats for the pursuit began and Kieran and his very new pilot, David Edwards, were first up. They took on Kieran Murphy and Lachlan Glasspool over the 4000 m (16 laps) of the track. To watch tandems in action is an experience. The brute force needed to get them going and the speed with which they hurl around that track is awesome. Kieran and David rode as one. There was no head or body swaying, just pure muscle powering a machine, which flew past in a blur. Kieran lapped his opponent twice on the way to a time of 4:18.514. Would it be good enough to get him into the final, justify his comeback and send him and David off to the world titles in Italy and then possibly the Rio Paralympics?

The next pair on the track included the current world champions. Since Kieran's gold medal win at the London Paralympics in 2012, Oz Tandem had dominated this event and held the world record.

They were brilliant. Like Kieran and David, they were totally synchronised. Riders and bike mould into a single high-speed unit. Oz Tandem dominated their heat and won in 4:17.172, 1.34 seconds quicker than Kieran's time, and were now clear favourites to win their third consecutive pursuit national title and continue on to Rio.

One more heat to go. Would Kieran's time hold up? Would he get the chance to take on Oz Tandem for the gold later in the day? It did. The next best winning time was 4:23.859. Now came the wait for the great race.

Kerry was at the velodrome, the first time for her and Tania since their respective tandem gold medal wins 20 years earlier. Memories of punishing training regimes, injuries, accidents and nerve-wracking competition came flooding back. Kieran came over to quietly sit with us; Mr Cool, although we all knew what the upcoming final meant to him.

At last Modra/Edwards and Oz Tandem were in position for the race for gold. The track commentator came alive. He talked glowingly of the return of Modra, the 43-year-old South Australian champion, winner of five gold and four bronze medals from seven Paralympic Games between 1988 and 2012, and two Commonwealth Games silver medals. The veteran had returned to take on the new champs and regain the crown. The otherwise quiet crowd became vocal. The small band of Modra relatives near the start/finish line began to chant. Kerry chewed her nails.

They were off, two amazing units with all riders standing on their pedals for the first half lap. Modra and Edwards got the better of this and after lap one had a lead of a quarter of a second ... or a blink!

Every time the tandems crossed the start/finish line the race commentator called out the margins. 'Modra/Edwards up by 0.5 of a second.' Then 0.6 and 0.7. We thought they might break Oz Tandem. But then a roar as the NSW guns surged. Down to 0.5, 0.4, 0.3 ... the laps were running out. Still the Modra/Edwards unit powered on. We yelled. The crowd yelled. The last lap and still the margin was 0.3 – and too big even for Oz Tandem. Officially the time was 4:17.929 and a winning margin of a mere 0.42 seconds ... the time it took for you to read that last word!

The old dog had won. He was national champion again, and his dream was alive.

We hugged each other and Kerry on the way out. She looked a mess, but a happy one. She would lose her husband, and the kids would miss their dad, for the weeks he would be away. But she was proud.

After the gold medal presentation, Kieran spoke to a Cycling Australia reporter who had also noted that the men's tandem pursuit final had produced the race of the day with a nail-biting battle:

> It was a big surprise. We worked with some strategies today to see which worked best. We are excited to have come away with the win and that final was as exhilarating as it was nerve wracking. I think the time I had off after the Commonwealth Games has helped. It is the same story again and again. After every games you get that bug and you want to get back on the bandwagon.

After the race and on request from management, David and I got to ride on Oz Tandem's bike. I can't imagine that they would have liked it too much. They've got a brilliant bike, all carbon fibre and financed by sponsors. I don't know where it comes from, probably America. Management asked me how I liked the ride. I loved it. It's a more aerodynamic position. Because it's longer at the back the stoker can get down lower. Management said they would make us a bike like that and took our measurements. I was very excited when it arrived. However, it was a heavier steel bike, not carbon fibre like OTs, and most disappointing was that when I looked at it closer I could see that it wasn't quite right. They had taken the measurements of the bike we're currently riding, not Oz Tandem's. We basically had a replica of the unsatisfactory tandem we were riding already.

David returned home to Queensland and Kieran's next competitive event was the national para cycling road race held around Williamstown, South Australia, on 27 February.

I rode this with good friend Mike Hoile. In the road race we broke away from Oz Tandem and the peloton at the 40 km mark. We were told later that Oz Tandem wanted to get the other guys to work together, but apparently they refused to help out. Oz Tandem had a monster gear on and were catching us on the downhills. We were spinning out and rolling while they were powering along. They caught us and it came down to a sprint, which they won. They train well for the longer races and had more power in their legs in the last lap. I've never really done that well in road races, except in 2004 when I won with Robert Crowe. David's forte is road racing and maybe if I'd have raced with him we might have won. To be honest I enjoyed riding with Mike and I didn't want to challenge Oz Tandem too much. We all play mind games and if they had been beaten, they might have decided to lift their intensity or be more determined when we next meet. I want them to think that they have me covered. It's all about Rio now.

Meanwhile Oz Tandem was playing mind games too. Soon after their loss at the Nationals they tweeted:

> Pursuit final - 4 min 18.3 silver. Didn't go to plan. The front tyre was going down and rode the final 8 laps spongy. * Should still see us in selection for Worlds team to travel to Italy in March. Bigger (quads), better & faster in 2016.

Stoker Matt Formston had missed almost six months of training due to illness. In March 2015 he had contracted glandular fever and post viral fatigue followed. Oz Tandem had been playing quite a bit of catch up, but the pair could only improve as Matt grew stronger. Oz Tandem had left no stone unturned and had been enduring specialised altitude training in the hope it would lead them to gold in September.

David returned to Adelaide in early March to work with me at a pre-training camp before leaving for Italy and the world titles. After the debacle with the tandem bike, which was supposed to be a copy of Oz Tandem's superbike, we had sourced another older tandem that we had discovered underneath the track in the cage. Formerly raced by Kieran Murphy and Lachlan Glasspool, it was a Cycling Australia tandem with a big frame and we were happy with it. I had found a superior aerodynamic riding position. I could get into a position where I could rest my elbows on the existing handlebars, put my forearms under David's seat and hold on to the top tube there. This meant I reached through right between his legs and folded my hands over so that they didn't brush against his legs. It was a little precarious and not as stable, but it did cut down wind resistance. Instead of my chin sometimes poking into the small of David's back, my head was now down behind his bottom, aerodynamic but not necessarily a nice place to be!

David was getting used to the new bike:

> Ultimately it would be better because it fitted Kieran as well. I needed to find the line again. When we started, I was all over the place, up and down the track, but I got it together for the Nationals. The disk wheels on this new tandem threw the line out again because you needed to force the wheel against the air current. And Kieran wasn't as stable because his arms were straight out in front of him. It was more difficult now, but we shaved off 0.1 second per lap!

Oz Tandem was like a thorn in my side. But it was good. It would make me better. In the past being unaware of the potential of overseas teams meant I had to create a phantom rider to chase. But these guys were here. For us to be assured of going to Rio, we had to beat Oz Tandem. If we were to lose to them, our only chance would be a wildcard entry. There were only four tandem positions available overall and we knew that the selectors always took a chance for gold over an assured silver. But this was risky. We just had to beat Oz Tandem, who were focusing on the pursuit as well. We didn't even want to know if there was any team in the world presently challenging our times.

Velodrome Fassa Bortolo in Montichiari, northern Italy, had hosted the 2011 UCI Para-cycling Games Track World Championships. There were to be 31 events decided over four days of competition across individual pursuit, time trial, scratch race, sprint and team sprint. The Australian team settled in well and enjoyed an excursion to look over Montichiari's local castle, Castello Bonoris, before the racing started. But the team was generally disappointed when it was their turn to train at the velodrome. The organisers there struggled to meet even minimal expectations.

When we first arrived, we were training in the dark. There was a little natural light, but we had to ask them to turn the lights on so that we could train safely. Then we couldn't practice using the starting gates because they didn't want to use the gas that operates these. The track needed to be heated, but we discovered that they only turned on those heaters for the competition.

Despite this I enjoyed riding there. I struggle with the Adelaide track because it's got sharp bends, which means you get a lot more whip out of the bends. That's okay, but to me it feels like you are always going downhill and then uphill into the straights. It's just a different style. I really liked the track in Italy. It had much bigger bends and I was able to pedal more evenly all the way around. David brought stability to the bike because size-wise he and I were evenly matched. David enabled me to work harder because I could put movement into the bike and he ironed that out.

Even when we were training, we were kept apart from Oz Tandem. We had different coaches. Jason wasn't training them. We trained at different times to avoid any chance of confrontation.

We had no idea how they were going and what times they were putting down.

But both teams knew that it was a head-to-head battle. The day arrived. More important for Kieran than a win in their heat was the time, because the two fastest teams were to ride off in the gold medal race. Oz Tandem easily won their heat in a time of 4:17.222. This was now the target for David, Kieran – and Rio.

David and I both felt great and we blitzed around the track in 4:12.568, a dramatic difference of 4.5 seconds. Rio was now assured, but in another dramatic twist the Spanish team of Ignacio Avila Rodriguez and Joan Font Bertoli flew around in 4:12.528 and narrowly bettered our time. The teams from Great Britain and Canada pushed Oz Tandem back to fifth place and out of medal contention.

Elated at our time, we left the velodrome and went back to the accommodation for lunch and a talk. We didn't speak about the Spanish at all. Beating Oz Tandem meant that we were on the plane to Rio! Between races we tend to shut down anyway. You don't want to be thinking of the next race because that can be wearing. It's irritating because you need to stay immobile, relaxed and as stress free as possible. I'm used to it, but David's been mainly a road cyclist, so he gets annoyed and impatient.

I was impressed with our coach Jason Niblett, who was doing a good job. He evaluated each effort in training and cut training back if he noticed fatigue. Before the final against the Spanish, Jason got us worried. He started by telling us to keep to our schedule, but after checking the qualifying times of the Spanish, he frowned and changed his mind. 'Bugger the schedule. Just give it all you've got!' was his final advice.

We decided to take a big risk – a big gear. In our qualifier in Italy we rode a 114" gear, which means for every rotation of the pedal, the wheel covers 114 inches (2.9 m) of track. In London, we rode a 108" gear after trying 110" without success. When we got to the final in Montichiari we discussed whether we should try an even bigger gear. Jason said that we had done everything we needed to do on the trip (i.e. qualify for Rio) and we wouldn't get another chance to experiment against competition like this, so why not. So we bumped it up to 116" knowing that the result was going to be gold or silver, so good either way. It is always more difficult to start in a higher gear, just like trying to start a car in fourth, but once you get rolling and provided you have the leg strength and stamina, you can cover the ground better. The sports scientists say that you don't blow the cardio-vascular system or go into oxygen deficit as quickly riding a bigger gear.

The Spanish are renowned for tandem racing and had often been my major opposition in the bigger championships. But I hadn't raced this team before.

Spanish stoker Ignacio Avila Rodriguez had an athletics background, winning a silver medal in the men's 4 x 400 m relay in the Sydney Paralympics and a gold medal in the men's 800 m in Athens. In Beijing, he had collected a bronze medal in the men's 1500 m. So here was an endurance athlete of some note.

In the final we expected to be slow from the gates and were surprised and delighted to take an early lead. At the kilometre mark our lead was out to 0.8 of a second, but we were worried because the Spanish have a good backend to their races. They come home well. So we decided to try to keep something in reserve to counter this. We didn't expect to be leading so comfortably.

Over the next 2 km we extended our lead, heading into the final kilometre with a two second advantage as we powered home to claim gold in 4:12.324, over four seconds faster than Spain and just over a second outside the world record held by Matt Formston and Mick Curran (4:11.213) at altitude in Aguascalientes, Mexico.

I was euphoric and surprised. I honestly didn't think we could go so fast. We could only hypothesise about what had happened to the Spaniards in the final. When there are two bikes on the track you have a choice, either to keep to your own planned schedule where your coach can give you each lap time and you keep to the plan, or the coach can look across the track and create a schedule based on your opposition. I think the Spaniards abandoned their plans and tried to match us. We went out reasonably hard and took their fast finish away from them. A rider cannot accelerate the tandem single-handedly; it must be a combined effort. We can't communicate through a race because we are on the limit, breathing hard and trying to focus through crowd noise, so we talk before the race and plan our tactics then. At the Worlds we experimented. In the first race, we just went flat out from the start and suffered at the end. We produced a much better time later with a more controlled and slower start for a 20 second lap . We then settled into a rhythm lapping at 15.5 seconds. We had decided that with six laps to go we would pour on the pressure and give it all we had to the finish line. It worked and we nearly reclaimed the world record.

When the Spaniards tried to increase their stroke, they managed briefly, but their energy was spent. It was noticeable that when they beat our qualifying time to get into the gold medal race, they really celebrated. It meant that they were going to Rio – and perhaps psychologically that is all they set out to do.

The strange thing was that we felt so good after the final and despite being only one second off the world record, we could have gone again. This was a surprise because after the qualifying race we were exhausted and happy to dismount.

In Italy, we still had the sprints to complete and we qualified eighth. This meant that we needed to beat my Glasgow nemesis Neil Fachie and Peter Mitchell from Great Britain to progress further. We didn't and the Fachie–Mitchell duo went on to claim another sprint gold.

Interestingly other teams were watching us. We had a French guy filming our pits area to see how we get ourselves organised before the race.

The Canadian stoker was sitting next to me before the medal presentation. I knew he was 44, my age. He cheekily asked, 'What training do you do? I haven't seen you at any of the recent championships. How can you get this good so quickly?' I told him that I'd been to the recent Commonwealth Games and that seemed to satisfy his curiosity.

Leaving Montichiari with 18 medals, of which eight were gold, Great Britain finished top of the medal table, followed by China (13 medals, six gold) and Australia (14 medals, five gold). Peter Day, Para-cycling Performance Director and Head Coach Cycling Australia was happy with the team:

> The overall standard was very impressive with all nations ramping up as the intensity builds towards the Rio 2016 Paralympic Games. There were several international breakthrough performers who will definitely be in the mix for team nomination to the Australian Paralympic Team.

We were looking forward to being home. We had good team morale at the Worlds, but the selection process for Rio put everyone under pressure and on edge. The two days after the racing were difficult because some people were elated, but many were very disappointed. To get to this level involves a lot of training and pain and for many failure here meant the end of their dreams.

* * *

What a surprise! At the age of 44, I was riding faster than at any time in my sporting career. I was trying to work out why. I can only think that it was because I'd changed my pedalling action, from just pushing down to creating a more circular motion. I now pulled my legs up and then stroked over the top to make a full rotation. I probably learnt this from the training for the Glasgow sprints. In the gym I was shown how to strengthen all the leg muscles and not only those used for pushing down on the pedals. My training partner, Mike Hoile, does a lot of this, so it helped to work out with him. It was incredible to find this extra power after all those years of cycling. It was like adding a couple of extra cylinders.

We were happy with our 'new' bike. Psychologically we knew we could do excellent times on it, but they'd have to replace all the cranks. We had issues with them at the Worlds. They were starting to come loose and the bottom bracket, or where the crank fits into the bike, was rounding off. We could feel it slipping with our starts, and any 'slop' means inefficiency.

I used to really struggle with helmets – well not so much the helmet, but the visor. I did a lot of training with the wind in my face and it gave me the satisfaction and sensation of speed. With the visor down, I felt zoned out. I didn't feel like I was in the race, rather like I was in a car. But in this new position I didn't get a lot of buffering wind anyway, so I was happier with my aero helmet.

I have nothing but praise for David Edward's dedication to the task and thoroughly enjoyed his company at the Para-cycling World

Titles, a new experience for him. I enjoy riding with different pilots, who get the opportunity to experience a tandem and the Games. I relish their enthusiasm. David's a different rider to Scott and any of my former pilots. He brought different strengths, so again there was the challenge of adapting.

Pilots of vision-impaired stokers have added responsibilities and David was not always aware of my blindness, and that I needed sighted help. I wanted him to have a good experience of his newfound sport, so I didn't make a fuss when he forgot my disability. Sometimes working with a disabled person is like being tethered at the hip; it can be frustrating. When I couldn't see him, especially in airports, I would just latch on to another group. I assumed management would clarify his role as carer before Rio. Having said that, we got along well and spent most of our overseas time together, often talking about tactics and expectations and always being mindful of staying positive. We hung on to the race for as long as possible, motivating us to keep going and aim for new heights.

Probably an even bigger surprise than the one-sided final against the Spaniards, was the performance of Oz Tandem. They were the reigning world champions, holding the world record. To miss out on being in the race for any medal was a shock to many. They were a brilliant team with such a clear and stated focus on success in Rio. Oz Tandem expected to win at the Worlds. They were doing similar times at the Nationals, but they didn't improve on this. Meanwhile we improved by five seconds.

It wasn't long after the team arrived back from Italy that a rumour began. It was soon verified on the Oz Tandem website. After many years of success, Oz Tandem had split. Pilot Mick Curran did not want to ride anymore. Matt Formston had found a new pilot, Nicholas (Nick) Yallouris.

David and I had thought we had seen off the Oz Tandem challenge this time. Not so! The old Oz Tandem had gained enough points to be in the Rio squad. David and I would have to race them again, albeit with a fresh face. That was a good outcome for Matt and for us, healthy competition.

Nick Yallouris would be 22 when he rode with Mick in Rio, so he was young. Coming from a BMX background, Nick had been cycling for seven years and had consistently won many state titles on both the road and track. Growing up on the central NSW coast, he was based close to Mick and according to their website, they trained together up to 13 times a week.

I was not surprised that Matt so quickly matched up with Nick and I had great respect for the potential of a new Oz Tandem. Nick was a talented cyclist with international tandem experience. Nick, riding with Paul Kennedy in the last world title sprints, had beaten us and won the Kilo title at the 2016 national titles, so we knew he could ride. Nick was an all-rounder. He had a history of racing well over longer distances on the single bike. He had a bit of length to his training and performance. We just didn't know what the new Oz Tandem was capable of. We wouldn't have to wait long to find out. The element of uncertainty is good and bad. If you don't know what to expect, then you train harder to overcome that doubt.

Kieran's eyes were getting worse and he was losing more forward vision. He was seeing more and larger spots covering words. It was harder for him to cross roads and when he rode a single bike, he liked to be in a group.

I didn't like riding singly anymore. Maybe I was showing a maturity and wisdom gained through bitter experience. About a month out from the Games I got really nervous. Wherever I went I took extra care especially when I was riding on a single bike and I could only hope that my pilot was doing the same. The margins were so close. Even a sprained ankle could be the difference between medalling and missing the finals. Once we reached our destination, management were very careful with hygiene and anyone who was ill was quarantined from the rest of the team.

I was somewhat spooked by a new phenomenon. My preparation for Rio had been short and sweet, and without incident. I was aware of this. For the last five Games, something major had always happened in the lead-up, but this time all was going well. This was exciting, because now I could see what I could do.

Scott Walsh of the Advertiser *tempted fate when he wrote:*

> Kieran Modra has never had a smoother preparation for a Paralympic Games, and the flawless lead-in has him concerned. 'I haven't had to deal with any trauma or accidents,' the veteran of seven Games said, grinning. 'When I rode with my wife in 1996 we had a crash the day before the race and in 2000 my preparation was too intense. I had court issues in 2004 and team issues in 2008, and then crashed before London. So this time, instead of worrying about those things, I am almost panicking. Have I taken all the steps and is everything in place on the track?' Kieran remained unsure whether this year's campaign would be his last. But, regardless, he was out to prove he was no spent force. 'I remember in London I felt a bit selfish standing up there on the podium for the third time in a row,' he says. 'This time most of the competitors are half my age so I'm thinking if they can't knock me off, I'm not going to hand it

> over to them. I'll give them something to chase and let people know that life doesn't go downhill after 40.

I didn't have to wait long.

On a Saturday afternoon in June, only hours before catching up with David at a special week-long training camp organised for us both, and 88 days out from Rio, I broke my jaw. I was riding my mountain bike on a pretty bad stretch of road near Salisbury, 45 km away from home on a solo training ride and ... I ran into the back of a stationary vehicle. I was lucky that it was a ute [utility truck], because once I hit it at 30 kph I somersaulted through the air, collected the tailgate with my head, landed in the back tray of the ute, and my bike landed on top of me. The thump was so loud that people in the local houses came running out to see what had happened. The driver of the parked ute was nearby, so he drove me to the local Lyell McEwin hospital, but there were many waiting. Darren and Tammy took me to the Royal Adelaide Hospital. Fortunately, I arrived at a 'quiet time', and the surgeons operated on the jaw almost immediately. They inserted plates and pins with rubber bands to help support the jaw. It would take six weeks to heal fully, with the pins removed after two weeks. I was restricted to eating soup, progressing to soft foods once the screws were out.

Other than a broken jaw I had four stitches in my lip, a corked quad and lots of bruises and scratches. Breaking my jaw was probably the best break to get. If it had been a collarbone (again) or a leg, it would have been a lot harder to get back into training. This time I didn't do too much damage to the car, but my mountain bike needed new forks and a new front wheel for starters and wasn't worth fixing.

Two days after the accident Kerry drove me to the velodrome

to see David and to talk to our coach, Jason. David was just back from a successful stint in Europe. To prepare for Rio without me he would work hard off the bike, and ride a single bike to stay fit.

Jason gave Kieran a training program that would have him back on the ergo on Thursday with the possibility of riding at the velodrome with David the following Sunday, shortly before he headed back to Queensland. Kieran wrote to me in June 2016:

> The jaw is going well. Got the stitches out on Monday. I had quite a beard till then, so am feeling much like myself now. It was such a relief to get back on the tandem. For starters, I didn't want to waste the time that David was here. We were pleasantly surprised just how good the bike felt, the position, the freshness in my legs (well they should be with so much time off). We rode both the track bike and the road tandem on the track. I've never ridden the road bike on the track before but we did because we had to know the position was okay. This bike was brought in from interstate and was the tandem Scott and I used in London for the road race and the road time trial (we broke the chain right on the start line so did not complete). We rode 5 km behind the motorbike with both tandems, but on the road tandem we had to be mindful not to use the brakes and to slow down gradually like a track bike would do. This was important because we had a couple of other riders with us on track bikes.
>
> I'm now focusing all my training on an ergo. I had a session this morning for 90 minutes. They are very good training tools while you have good motivation. If you haven't it is very hard to push into the lactic threshold. I did a minute at 400 watts followed by a 30 second rest. Did this five times. Ten minutes rest and did it again twice more. You always picture the race where you want to see yourself, on top spot on the podium, and you imagine what it will feel like. I can understand athletes

disappointment when they don't win, because that is all you think about.

For much of July, David and Oz Tandem would be training in Italy without Kieran. The next time Kieran would see David would be in Italy on 12 August. Meanwhile Kieran would train at home and this troubled him.

Being with my family is important to me, as was getting to spend time with Darren. However, I was keenly aware that David and the new Oz Tandem were training in Europe. While Adelaide was experiencing a wet June, the southern Europeans had blue skies and sunshine. I would have loved to be with them.

An old injury had returned and was giving me some grief. I'd got a bit of a tennis elbow, so I couldn't even kite surf. It even hurt to tat. It was the old javelin injury and I needed to sort it out. Not being able to lift weights meant I did a lot of core work.

Aware that my opposition might be gaining advantage from my own inconveniences in the lead-up to Rio, I created a challenge for myself. Because I was now moving too quickly and therefore dangerously on a road bike, I started riding a mountain bike. It was significantly heavier and so when I rode with the road bikers, I worked harder just to keep up. Instead of generally being up the front, now I was hanging on to the tail following wheels. Some of the road bikers got a little annoyed that I was keeping up with them, but it was all in good fun. It was another way that I could go above and beyond what my competitors were expecting me to do.

I was previously riding blocks of 100 km three times a week on my road bike on top of my ergo sessions. When I changed to my mountain bike, I couldn't ride those distances at first, but after a while I managed and sometimes I even rode 150 km. On Tuesday,

Thursday and Saturday mornings I rode my mountain bike slowly to Mike Hoile's place and then we got on a tandem and generally rode around 100 km. In between it was ergo work programmed by my coach, which I could do at SASI or at home. For Rio we wanted to change the gearing again, so I wanted to get stronger still and therefore rode a lot of hills.

I enjoy riding because I can. I can ride up a hill, and the next one, and the one after that ... there is a feeling of invincibility. The race itself is the enjoyable part. You are riding on fresh legs. The masseurs have given you a good massage. You've had that tapering period and you come into the race feeling a million bucks. It's all the training and grinding preparation that's difficult.

We were expecting the Spanish to be better performed in Rio and to backup better between the qualifying rounds and the final. What surprised us most when we beat them last was the time. In London we did a 4:17.756, and at the Worlds we did a 4:12.324. I was expecting competition to be tough in Rio and looking forward to the challenge and maybe even a world record.

It didn't go to plan.

15

Rio and the black line

2016

Rio de Janeiro is an experience in itself. Scenically nestled between the Brazilian highlands and a glorious Atlantic coastline, it is a confronting mixture of famous beaches like Copacabana and Ipanema, the 38 metre high Christ the Redeemer statue atop Mt Corcovado, Sugarloaf – a granite monolith with cable cars to its summit – and sprawling favelas, or shanty towns.

When announcing the team, chef de mission of the 2016 Australian Paralympic team Kate McLoughlin said at the Adelaide Super-Drome that Australia's cycling team would aim to cement itself as one of the world's very best:

> The talent on this team is enormous, which is evident in the fact that nearly every athlete has won either a Paralympic or World Championship medal. I'm confident that the 2016 cycling team is one of the strongest Australia has ever produced, and I'm looking forward to seeing the team aim for a top three finish on the track, and to be amongst the top ten in road cycling.

Since Atlanta in 1996, Australia had won 34 gold, 24 silver and 26 bronze medals at the Paralympic Games in para-cycling. In London, Australia achieved 14 medals, six of which were gold. The team had a target to beat.

One of the advantages of the Paralympics following on from the Summer Games is that some of the issues with the venue have been sorted. On arriving to substandard accommodation for their Summer Games squad, the Australian Olympic Committee announced that they would relocate athletes to better hotels. Almost immediately extra maintenance staff and more than 100 cleaners were deployed. An exasperated Rio Lord Mayor's quip that maybe the Aussies would like kangaroos brought in to make them feel more at home was returned by Australian chef de mission Kitty Chiller when she replied, 'We would rather have a plumber!'

However, when the Australian Olympic cycling team took to the track expecting to win four or five medals, they finished with a disappointing solitary silver and bronze, after being dominated by Team GB (Great Britain). Cycling Australia high performance manager Kevin Tabotta promised a full-scale review of its track underperformance. He admitted to Reece Homfray of the Herald Sun on 16 August 2016 that the high-performance program had misjudged the overseas training camps in Los Angeles and Mexico and the taper period leading into the Games. Kevin stated:

> Clearly one nation moved ahead of the rest and made some significant gains in a short period and we weren't able to match that. Great Britain has been the masters of being on world level at world championships and within four months stepping (up) at a rate that is two to three times any other nation. That's what they've done in the last three cycles, I'm sure there are performance directors and coaches out there who would love to have the blueprint. They've (GB) got it and have used it to great effect. We need to master an August peak and we haven't nailed that yet.

Kevin denied that the British Team's superiority came from its greater population and lottery funding. He added:

> If there's anything in that message, it's sometimes you have to go slower to go faster ... We just have to find a way to deal with the AIS and athletes to see how we can ramp into an Olympic Games, manage expectations and be happy with fourths and thirds (at world titles) along the way, knowing our athletes will be supported on the way through to gold.

On arriving at the Australian para-cycling training camp in Montichiari, Italy, one of the first experiences I enjoyed was an inspiring talk given by Brad McGee, an Australian Olympian and cycling coach. Having just been to Rio, Brad could relay insights into Olympic Village life and left all with the mantra: 'Enjoy every moment and every metre.'

But I had some catching up to do. When my jaw was wired, I had lost weight. I ate a lot of soup, pureed salad and bizarrely, pureed steak. Kerry did a wonderful job looking after me. She always does. She gets me back riding after all the accidents and injuries and it can't be an easy job. She is wonderful, but I had lost condition.

The accident with the ute had affected my self-confidence. It's not what I see that worries me. It's what I can't see. I don't want to give up riding a single bike, but I need to come to terms with the fact that my sight is deteriorating, meaning my world is shrinking and my limitations increasing. It's affecting my independence and confidence and I get another insight into what Holly is going through. But I must keep pushing forward and be strong for my girls.

We were accommodated about two kilometres from the velodrome and we generally rode our bikes there or we did a warm-up loop of about 30 minutes, so that we were ready for action when we got to the track. The hotel was quite good. We'd been there before, but this time they'd roomed everyone separately. I wasn't in a room with David and although this gave us more space, it did get a little lonely. I didn't get to talk to David much at all, unless we met downstairs in the lobby.

David needed quiet time:

> I enjoyed rooming with Kieran and we did that in Rio. However, I needed to study to get my university degree and being in a single room helped. Coming over here for three weeks with Oz Tandem and others before Kieran was good and bad. It provided data to the trainers on what worked better, because both preparations had been so different. And I think it was good for mental preparation. Three months was a long time to be with one person and there was the chance that we would get tired of being together and fed up with the training regime. It was great to see Kieran arrive and we were very keen to train and ride.

Our track sessions were often short and intense and we had a few long road rides up into the mountains, which were challenging with lots of switchbacks and 10% inclines and hard work, but exhilarating as well. We did one climb that I'd be happy not to do again. It was 5 km at 13%, which took us about a half hour averaging 9 kph. It felt like the bike was going to stall and it was relentless going up and up. We didn't have to go down it because we descended on the other side of the mountain. This had its own drama because when you descend for a longer period, the brakes heat up the rim and this can pop the tyre. We stopped halfway down to let the brakes cool down. The wheels were so hot that you couldn't touch them for more than a second.

But we had mishaps. We were riding on the track and we had a blowout on the front disc wheel. It was on the bend and we were going reasonably fast, and it threw us up the track. From experience, I knew instantly that with a blown front tyre, it was very unlikely we could hold the bike up. But full credit to David. I have not known anyone to be able to hold a bike up like he did. He managed to get us to the bottom of the track, which took us two laps of gradually descending so that the front wheel wouldn't slip out on us. I could hear the carbon fibre disc crunching as the rim was being flattened. It was such a relief to come to a stop. The fear of crashing is always in the back of your mind, especially since I have had my share. But you don't dwell on this. You've got a job to do; to keep pushing the boundaries, and so we were back at it soon after, on the limit again.

Something far worse happened two days later. It was a double day; track in the morning and again in the afternoon. In the morning session we had to ride hard behind the motorbike and then sit off that and do another eight laps. I've found this tough on my legs and after each day I'm ready for bed at 9 o'clock. All our training now is high-end and we are pushing at boundaries. It was our last effort for the session and we were giving it everything, at 60 kph.

David recalls what happened next:

> It happened so quickly. There was a pop and the next second I was sliding. I didn't want splinters so I tried to roll my body. I think that stopped me quicker as well and then I was just sitting there in disbelief. Usually it is easier to hold the bike up with a rear wheel problem compared to something going amiss with the front tyre. The g-forces at that point of the track were so great that we didn't even have a chance. I came out of it with a bruised hip, a few burns, but thankfully no splinters.

Somehow David, nearer the front, slid to the track – but I came down with a thump. Crashing down on my thigh and spinning off towards the fence, I braced myself for significant injury. When we had both stopped sliding and I tried to stand, I was aching from hip to knee and had no strength in my knee. My kit was torn and ripped and I had many nasty burns, but my main concern was that my leg had shut down and I could only hobble.

Diagnosed as a severe corked leg, the only cure was rest. It was similar to Kerry's accident in Atlanta and the muscle just clamped up, but Kerry had the added problem of the handlebars digging into the muscle. Because Kieran impacted and slid, a much thinner layer of muscle was damaged and so he was able to recover more quickly.

I have a better idea of the pain that Kerry suffered to win gold in Atlanta. After lying in bed and using ice to reduce the swelling for hours at a time, I became restless and decided to catch the team car to the velodrome to support David's ergo session. It was a mistake. I shouldn't have gone out to the track. I should have stayed back at the hotel and rested. It wasn't good mentally. To sit and watch the other boys tearing around the track, I just didn't want to watch it. I moved into the foyer and waited for the session to finish. I could see our preparation disappearing into the distance and it nearly broke me.

David was more philosophical about the accident:

> If the tyre hadn't blown then, it would have blown later and possibly in a race. It was shit timing, but we'd had a lot of shit thrown at us over the last few months. There was Kieran's jaw, but we couldn't do anything about it. We just needed to adapt to it and do what we could. We couldn't be afraid of having another crash because that would mess us up. So, we put that crash out of our minds and dived into the corners confidently. We had two more weeks to regain our confidence.

Two days after the accident and we were getting back into full swing with a double track session morning and afternoon. I was sore, but gradually feeling better and more energised. The mechanical issues continued as we broke the cluster, the rear cogs on the bike. One of the cogs wasn't strong enough and folded against the next cog. The mechanics said it was a design fault and the cluster was too light.

I was healing well but training hit another hiccup. I'd had headaches for the previous two days and woke with vertigo and poor balance. I had trouble controlling my left side. My legs were weak and light and my left hand was numb. Confused and worried because I'd never had anything like this before, I hobbled off to Dr Geoff Verrall, who had only arrived the night before. He was the doctor who had given me the all-clear for London after the crash into a car. It was a great comfort to have him there and to sit down and speak with him. I was stressing and he relaxed me.

Replays of the crash show that I threw out my left arm to protect myself and I must have stretched some tendons before I was thrown across the track. The muscles in the area had moved in to protect the tendon damage, likely causing the numbness. The medics had cleaned up the wounds immaculately to avoid infection and had been massaging my neck and shoulders in an attempt to relax those strained muscles.

On the following day, even though I wasn't 100%, I felt like I had to get out on the bike. We explored for nearly three hours, enjoying the fresh air and the countryside. It energised us both. It was important that Dave and I stay connected. I felt that it was worth an extra 5% in races ... to work for each other.

I got back to Montichiari tired, and had trouble sleeping. With the headaches at night, sometimes with double vision, and the workload, I wasn't feeling perky. Dave was also getting over a cold and had a niggling cough. And we were having problems with our racing line. We'd been too high on the track and when we were told of this, we didn't believe them until we saw the replays and video from the world titles. We put a camera on the front of the bike and we could see how far off the black line we were. It is most important to be smooth, but we needed to take the shortest and quickest route – the way of the black line, imprinted by following the path of the motorbike.

Having Oz Tandem in Montichiari was unnerving for both of us, especially me. I wanted to be affable, but there was no getting around the fact that we were in direct competition. Oz Tandem was going well and covering a lot of road miles; we were having challenges. We hadn't done any road rides with them and on the track we did different sets. I think it was a good idea because I was sure that even on a road ride, the competitiveness would have surfaced with both teams keen to outdo the other. I was curious to find out how David had gotten along with Matt and Nick from Oz Tandem in the weeks before I arrived.

David was less concerned:

> It's a big team here and although the team dynamics are good, we don't all have to be best friends. In Lavinia, I was living in the same apartment with Matt and Nick and although I chatted with them both, especially Nick, we didn't train together. We're not chatting much now. I'm still more concerned about Britain and Spain. It's good to have the Oz Tandem boys here because they're real and we know we have to focus just to beat them.

Before the crash, we were riding good times; 15.5 second laps, just as we wanted. In the last few days at Montichiari we were encouraged with some outstanding training sessions. When I walked up the ramp and into the velodrome my legs felt tired and heavy, but once on the bike I was energised. We were knocking out lap times of 15.1 and 15.0, which was incredibly reassuring.

The doctors were confident that feeling would slowly return to my left fingers. I'd been doing some tatting and giving Dave some little pieces. After a last road ride of 80 km the road bike was packed and we were ready to leave. Despite all the setbacks, I was fairly laidback about Rio. After all it was my eighth Paralympic Games.

For David it was a new experience:

> We'll be in Rio soon and I don't know what to expect. I am just trying to keep an open mind. To go in flexibly and see what happens. I'm not worried about the track there or what the Rio organisation has put in place. I'm worried about what we can control and our form on the day.

Word had got back to the training camp that all was not going well with the organisation of the Paralympics. Keren Faulkner, the team's manager of performance services and physical therapies, was already in Rio and trying to prepare the athlete's Village for the cycling squad's imminent arrival. She messaged the team:

> We've just started unpacking the Australian team gear. Rio workforce, who had initially promised to help us unpack, move beds etc haven't shown up. This doesn't matter at the moment but what it could indicate is that some of the services we might be expecting during Games time could be a bit compromised. If our team can be positive and resilient then I think this could be to our advantage – I'm sure we can deal with this better than others. There are lots of positives in the Village and it's

> going to be a lovely place to prepare for competition. Please be prepared for surfaces that are a bit uneven, a reasonable walk to the dining hall, and not being able to flush toilet paper at all (!). This last one is important – it's in your best interests to stick to this.

On ABC's Radio-National news on 22 August the crisis of under-funding was mentioned. Reportedly only 12% of tickets had been sold and in a desperate bid to save money Rio Paralympic organisers planned to close at least one venue and media facility, shed staff and shrink stadium capacities. The reporter went on to say that ten countries would struggle to get athletes to the Games because promised travel grants had not been paid on time.

Chef de mission, Kate McLoughlin, was quick to respond and assured listeners that funding for the Australian Paralympic squad was in place and that the Committee had already written to Brazil to see what cuts had been made. If a shortfall affected the athletes in any way, the Australian Committee would ensure the athletes would not be adversely affected. The Australian athletes were a resilient bunch and would enjoy whatever Rio put up. From a performance point-of-view, Australian athletes had never been better, or better prepared. Kate wanted this team to cement fifth spot on the medal tally ... a position achieved since the Games in Barcelona. But anything could happen, a lot of countries were vying for that top five position.

Russia had lost its appeal to the Court of Arbitration for Sport to overturn a decision by the International Paralympic Committee to ban the nation's 267-strong team from the Games after revelations of systematic doping. This opened the way for the Australian squad to grow from 170 to 176 members, the biggest assembled for an overseas Games. Kate McLoughlin was obviously delighted to be taking more athletes to Rio, but was quick to point out that the Paralympic and

Olympic teams were so totally different that it would be unfair to draw comparisons.

When Kitty Chiller and the Australian Olympic team arrived back in Australia on 24 August with eight gold medals and 29 in total, its worst haul since Barcelona in 1992, she pointed out that over half the team were Olympic rookies and just under half were less than 25 years of age, and that this augured well for the 2020 Games in Japan. Prime Minister Malcolm Turnbull and Governor-General Peter Cosgrove made stirring welcome home speeches. However, many Australians were feeling a sense of disappointment, perhaps because the expectations of the team were high and probably unrealistic. Once again the Australian public's high expectations shifted to their Paralympic team.

* * *

I decided to keep a diary during my time in Rio.

31/8/16 Wednesday

Arrived at the airport at 5 am feeling very tired. The bikes were loaded onto the bus by Brazilians, who I'm sure didn't realise how many bikes they had to fit in. They panicked but eventually managed. We had to wait outside of the Village and finally we were shown in, but not without a meeting with the chef de mission and staff. We were based on the 16th floor of a 19-storey apartment block. Each floor housed 24 people in four apartment units. After checking our rooms, the first place we visited was the dining hall. David was in awe of the food selection and size of the facility. I think we both gorged ourselves a little at lunch. We went to the basement to put together our road bikes and spent 17 minutes getting to the track by bus. Later we realised we could ride to the track in about ten minutes. The track bikes were all put together by the mechanics and we were able to have a light ride around the track for 45 minutes. I was so tired from the flight and lack of sleep that I had the best night's sleep ever!

I emailed Uncle Andy:

> The only difficulty with our accommodation is with the lifts. There are three lifts for the entire building and with so much traffic we spend a lot of time waiting for the lifts. Overall I'm quite impressed. There are a lot of stories going around and there were teething problems, but we have a pool and deckchairs. We can't put paper in the toilets because the pipes are too narrow and they block. The story is that the Irish used paper and when this blocked the pipe, they used sticks to remove the clog. But the sticks pierced the pipe and the sewerage escaped into the Americans below them. The food has been great. It is a huge food hall and is the centre of social activity and get-togethers. David really enjoys it there.

1/9/16 Thursday

David always likes to sleep in so I went to breakfast by myself. It's a little difficult because I can't see what there is on offer and that's why David is so helpful. He's never had to be a support person before, but he is thoughtful and does look out for me a lot. I take my hat off to him. My independence is not what it used to be and I look for support a lot more, especially in groups of people, in airports and velodromes. I can't recognise people anymore. It makes me feel sad, but I shrug it off and enjoy any company and pleasantries with the people who do approach me.

The road ride was cancelled because the traffic was very busy at the road course, so we rode around the Village on a designated path laid for this purpose. It was made of new concrete but not levelled so it was lumpy and uncomfortable to ride on. We went on a small road ride just out of the Village. We had clear instructions that didn't seem that clear once we left the Village. We didn't stay to the bike path all the time and there was some confusion among the riders where the turn-around was supposed to be.

After lunch we rode out to the track as a team and did a hard session on the track, a flying 2 km twice to get used to the track and to blow out the cobwebs. Peter Day allowed a camera on the tandem so that we could study our lines. We rode quite well and I felt good with the effort.

The Australian team was in for a shock. Australian gold-medal-winning cyclist Michael Gallagher had tested positive to a banned blood booster erythropoietin (EPO). He was immediately handed a mandatory provisional suspension by Cycling Australia and the Australian Paralympic Committee and sent home to Australia. The news was about to rock his fellow Aussie athletes.

2/9/16 Friday

I woke to the disturbing news about Michael Gallagher. The whole team was shocked. We had a team meeting at 7 am. I emailed Uncle Andy later that day:

> It was devastating. Everyone was stunned. When the news broke we had a meeting and no one could speak. You wouldn't expect anyone with that stature to do that. It was unbelievable, but it's happened and we need to move forward. Every athlete here has been chosen for a job and to make Australia proud. We've got to look past the negatives. I think that things have settled down now and the athletes are back on track and concentrating on their own events. I felt really bad for him.

Michael Gallagher later apologised using Facebook. He revealed there that he had turned to EPO because he was dealing with depression and the pressure of expectation. He claimed to have sourced the drug and injected himself. He further admitted to doing this before the Nationals in South Australia in February, before the world titles in Italy, and again before leaving for the Italian training camp in July.

2/9/16 Friday *(continued)*
We focused on the road ride today, splitting up into smaller groups. The course is very hard with short sharp climbs of around 16%, and on the back end of the course there is another gentle climb for 2 km. We do three laps. It is incredibly scenic as the course goes along the beach and then into the mountains. It's very pretty ... but I'm not looking forward to racing on it.

3/9/16 Saturday
Track work was at 10 am and we rode there as a group. We had to do 3 x 2 km standing starts. Initially I wasn't keen to go too hard, but later I found myself not being able to go hard. My legs were fatigued and our times showed something was wrong. David was good and going strong, but I was struggling to push to the end of the effort. The plan was to sit on 15.2 second laps, but we ended up doing 15.8 second laps and were getting slower. Jason, our coach, ended up pulling the pin on our last effort.

4/9/16 Sunday
Four days to go! My weight stands at 85.7 kg, which is great considering I've been drinking so much Coke. David did a road ride and I stayed back. David and I went to the rooftop of our building. I'm not sure if we're allowed, but the view over the Village was stunning. I was interviewed by the Australian press about the Michael Gallagher ban. I was worried about the questions, but in the end I was very happy with my responses. Our track session in the afternoon was at 4 pm and we rode the 4 km to the track.

Workmen were resurfacing the paintwork on the bike path so we had to go up a small ramp and suddenly stop. I went to quickly grab the railing and smacked my hand on the protruding prongs, puncturing the soft tissue near my thumb. It immediately swelled into a ball. With blood running from my hand we continued on to the track. The medics cleaned me up and bandaged my hand. It was sore and throbbing and made me feel achy but I still did the training sessions of 3 x 500 m flys at full pace. The girls sprint tandem was to follow us and they would try to come over us, so bets were laid. We did 14 sec per lap. We were very happy with that result even with a sore hand. I checked in with the medics at the Village and got some painkillers for the night.

Soon after Michael Gallagher's positive test for EPO, chef de mission Kate McLoughlin had been quick to tell the media that strict drug testing was a good thing and that none of the other athletes had been implicated. She warned that the athletes would obviously be subjected to some extra testing, which they would welcome, because everyone would then know they were clean. Kieran didn't have long to wait ... and it wasn't a comfortable experience:

5/9/16 Monday

86.7 kg, 3 days to go

Today was a total rest day for me. David went on a road ride this morning. I got my hand looked at and re-dressed by the team doctor. At around lunchtime I was approached by ASADA for a drug test. It took me ages to go to the toilet and so I drank heaps of water. We then had our flag-raising ceremony to welcome the Australian team to the Village. It was well done but I found myself looking for the toilet, as I wanted to go every five minutes.

I'm struggling a bit with the track. It is well finished, but the banking and corners are not like Montichiari's, more like Adelaide's. The longer straights and shorter bends increase the g-forces and it's harder to keep the bike down on that black line. Dave and I are sharing a room and we're getting along well. We are trying to get our legs freshened up, but more importantly we want to get our minds focused. We will get nervous and I'm not looking forward to that. I think this will be the hardest of all the Games I've been to. Have I still got the killer instinct? I'm not sure. What I want most is a gold medal for David. That's my driving force. He's enjoying it all and I'm getting a lot of enthusiasm from him. I've been doing some time lapse photography on the roof of the building with stunning results.

6/9/16 Tuesday

Track training today went from 11 am until 1 pm. We did a flying 2 km with good results. Jason was very happy with it. David must have done a lot of work because I'm still not keen to work flat out yet. We completed a three-lap hit out from a standing start. I did just enough without blowing my legs, but still not confident that my legs are coming good. David is looking confident and feeling really good. This worries me as I don't want to let the team down, so I'm telling him I'm going well, but in my mind I'm struggling.

Back at the Village I looked for another massage trying to freshen up my legs. Somehow they felt a little sorer and again I am questioning my readiness.

I've been missing meals over the last couple of days due to the fact I've been having long massages, have been on rides or just through laziness. The dining hall is quite a walk and we need to allow at least an hour.

7/9/16 Wednesday

85.9 kg

Made it to breakfast finally and enjoyed it. This was followed by an hour-long roll on the road tandem with Alistair and Kyle, with the support car following us along the time trial circuit. I'm still trying to freshen up my legs, but feeling a little sluggish and not wanting to push them over a 3 out of 10 effort level. We had another meeting, which is all we seem to do lately, talking about race numbers and how to handle the media when coming off the track after races. There were team photos in our formal get up and those going to the opening ceremony were clearly excited and getting ready to head to the rows and rows of buses ready to take them there. I had a massage and needed my hand attended to. It's healing and should be good to go tomorrow. I then had to walk the one kilometre to the food hall for dinner. I did this in my formal gear, feeling a little agitated, I guess because I am left behind from the Opening Ceremony – a driving force that would really get me going.

8/9/16 Thursday

Race day!

I only became nervous when we started talking about the race, otherwise I was reasonably relaxed. By ten all my gear was packed including gloves, race socks, helmets etc. We rode from the Village to the track and nearing the velodrome, we grew nervous again. At the last couple of training sessions I have been feeling sleepy, so today I was determined to keep the system active and started to roll the legs on the ergo. At this stage we had 90 minutes to go. The pressure and anticipation were building. I saw the other bikes ride but David didn't want to tell me their times because they were fast.

David was right! In the first of eight heats, Irish pair Damien Verecker and pilot Sean Hahessy had set a good time of 4:20.139. This was far and above the best effort until heat five, when Dutchmen Stephen de Vries and Patrick Bos set a new Games record of 4:14.258.

In the following heat Oz Tandem was up against the Dutchmen Vincent ter Shure and Timo Fransen. Matt Formston and Nick Yallouris were in front at the kilometre mark, but the Dutchmen powered home to set the world record at 4:09.527! Suddenly the bar had been lifted and to get into the medal rounds those yet to ride were going to have to ride personal best times around this new world record mark.

The Spanish team of Ignacio Avila Rodriguez and Joan Font Bertoli, runners-up at the recent Worlds, were up next. They lowered the time of Verecker and de Vries to move into second place, but came nowhere near the new world record. So with one heat and only two teams left, Vincent ter Shure and the Spanish pair knew they had qualified for the medal races to be held later in the evening.

Kieran and David were racing the British team of Steve Bate and Adam Duggleby. Kieran didn't know this as he waited for the start of the race, but if they were going to race each other again for gold, they would both have to go under Vincent ter Shure's new world record!

8/9/16 Thursday *(continued)*

Lining up to start was a surreal feeling. I have done it dozens of times before, but now I have a new position on the bike. I knew I had to go faster and I wasn't sure how good my legs felt. I was thinking: get this one out of the way and focus on the finals. The counter started and on zero we got a good start, but two pedal strokes out and I pulled my foot out of the pedal – a false start. In disbelief we rolled a lap back to the start line for a second attempt. The mechanic tightened the pedals and away we went. Eight laps in and I felt fine, strong and in control. I then started to feel a sense of anxiety as my legs were tiring and out of the corner of my eye I could see the Brits catching us – and I started to panic. At the world titles I had felt more power from David at this stage, which I could work off. But not now. Falling into despair over the last couple of laps I just waited for them to go by. Walking off the track I thought, Oh well, we'll do better in the finals. David said nothing to me as we walked through the media area; no one wanted to talk to us and I knew something was wrong. Then a media person told me our place. 'Sixth?' I said. 'With a time of 4.14?' I was overcome with shock, disbelief and panic. Where was my chair? How could I find it, because I didn't want to talk to anyone? We hadn't made the finals. Our race was run. David still had not said a word and after 45 minutes he wanted out of that building. I wasn't far behind. They say it takes time for things to sink in and the more it sank in, the more painful it felt, like sharp nails. On the ride back to the Village we didn't say a word. We finally got to the comfort of our rooms. I had never experienced anything like this before. There was no going back to the track for finals. The work we both had put in over the past ten months ... the crashes. Was I blaming David? I could feel myself doing it. He should have been able to go harder, but I knew I must not express that idea. He did everything he could. He was just as devastated as I was. Jason tried to comfort us, with little success. He started talking about the road time trial and tried to get us to focus on that, but I wasn't even listening.

We went to McDonalds and sat with the Polish tandem girls, and learnt how their tandem combination worked. We didn't want to talk to anyone in the Aussie camp, they would have tried to be positive. We needed time to grieve. Anyone would have thought someone had died. Winning is easy, but when you lose you evaluate everything. And I wonder, was it the fact we had to peak three times in nine months? For every ride we had to jump through hoops and take ourselves to breaking point. Maybe we just couldn't do it again? Was it that we had it too good in Italy with perfect track and ideal conditions, and then coming to a track that was difficult to ride and very different to what we had been training on? It's plausible.

Kieran and David had held the lead until the 1500 m mark. In a race very similar to Oz Tandem's heat six, the British turned up the pressure and the Australian pair couldn't go with them. Bate and Duggleby dominated the back end of the contest and took over a further second off the previous world record with a slashing time of 4:08.146. Kieran and Dave managed 4:14.339; sixth position and less than one second away from a ride-off for the bronze medal.

Out of the 12 medals on offer on the first evening of the track cycling program, almost all of them were won by cyclists from Great Britain, USA and the Netherlands. Australian Susan Powell won silver in the Women's C4 3000 m Individual Pursuit to deny those countries a clean sweep. This was a pattern often repeated over the cycling program, both on the track and on the road.

It is interesting to see at what stage the medallists in Kieran's race were up to at the world titles in Italy. In the event where Kieran and David clocked a 4:12.324 to win the title, Bate and Duggleby came fourth with a 4:16.555 (and were even slower in their race-off for bronze), ter Shure/Fransen came sixth with a 4:17.331, and de Vries/Bos seventh with a 4:17.875.

Where Kieran and David had been forced to peak in March to beat Oz Tandem and to get on the plane to Rio, the Great Britain and Netherlands teams had been building to peak in Rio. It worked!

9/9/16 Friday

I plucked up the courage to call Kerry. The family was all very good and supportive, but for once I didn't want to be heartened. I listened to their encouragement enough to get through the conversation and then went back to spending the day moping around with David. We had an ergo session getting ready for the time trial and I think it was good to be able to vent some of that frustration. I know David did.

By the end of the day I was feeling a little more settled. I couldn't believe how much this had affected me. With all my years of experience and success, suddenly I couldn't see a positive. Was I happy with my efforts? Did I do my best? I guess I'm still learning how to be an athlete. I felt a real sense of loss for David; I hadn't got a gold medal for him. I emailed Uncle Andy:

> I have no doubt you know the result of our race. It has been devastating and a big blow to our morale. Winning is easy, but going through this I guess showed me what passion I had for it. What worries me is I've taken a fall but I've brought David down with me. I'm working my way through it ... but David?
>
> We still have the time trial on the 14th and the road race three days later but our chances are slim. The Village is feeling a little like a prison with too much time to think.

I responded:

> Yes ... I stayed up all night here to watch your race on my computer ... and felt quite devastated for you and David. I posted the following message on Facebook: 'I'm sure that you are hurting, Kieran, but some of us know the setbacks that you've overcome just to be there. We also know that you will have taken this like the champion you are. You are a terrific mentor to so many people. Keep inspiring!' And many people responded to this.

But the hurting will be deep. Express your feelings so that you can get them out of your system and move on. In the meantime, enjoy the Rio experience as well as you can, give your remaining races your best shot and remember that Australia is proud of you both. You are a champion and just because things went wrong on one day it doesn't stop us remembering what success you've had and what you've done and are doing for people with disabilities.

The rest of the team is going well and needs your experience and encouragement.

Thanks for your honesty and you will always be a champion in my eyes.

I was endeavouring to lift Kieran's spirits, but that inspiration was to come from another source.

10/9/16 Saturday

At 9.30 am we went for a 2½ hour road ride – a lap of the road circuit and one of the time trial course. It was good for us to get out of the Village, even if we did have a car following us. I'm feeling a little better today, but sense David is still struggling.

I'm starting to talk to people about it; the struggle and pressure of the race. I feel my sporting career has been turned on its head. I feel disappointed that I haven't handled it better. After everything I've been through, why is this so hard? Surely lying in hospital is worse? But no, because there I had a challenge. Here I didn't just lose, but under-performed. Perhaps it is good for my family to see me like this because they know I am still struggling. I fear for the road races as the results will be much the same. I like to think we could turn it around, but I must start preparing for the reality.

Makala has just done her 800 m race at Santos stadium for the school competition. She was so nervous to the point she wanted to pull out. Kerry said to her, 'Run your own race for the first lap because the other girls will probably sprint away and see how you go in the second lap.' She was last after the first lap and realised she had more to give in the second and so started to pass the other runners. She passed nearly half the field to place ninth. I am so proud of her and very sad not to be there. I remember those days and being proud of my efforts. I feel I must remember those feelings and take comfort in my girls' performances. I can learn from them. Makala was able to walk away feeling content and that is what I have to do. I have nothing to prove. In fact the British rider we raced in the qualifying round said he was honoured to race with such a great icon in the sport.

I know now how Jan Mulder felt when I beat him in Athens, catching him in the finals. He had been the reigning champion. It is fair to pass the baton on to the next worthy opponents. But it's not that we lost that I'm most unhappy about, it's the fact we should have done better. I didn't realise how high the podium was, because it really hurts when you fall off (feels more like I've been pushed).

My role now is to get David back on track and back into that happy place. For him to put this experience up there with his mother passing really worries me. The Paralympics has so much to offer and he was really getting into it before our race. It's how we come back from this that defines us and I take solace in Makala's willpower to push and overcome her fears; that will inspire me.

11/9/16 Sunday

I've been trying to get David out of the rut. I decided we need to get out of the Village and go to venues and see the other sports. We rode to the track and watched Matt and Nick ride the Kilo. They came sixth in a strong field. David was quiet as we sat in the crowds. I think he's conjuring up negative thoughts. Watching the one-legged guys in the team sprint races always inspires me, but by the end of it I sensed David wanted to go back to the Village. At lunch we had a team gathering at the picnic tables in the recreational dining area. It gave us a chance to mingle with other teammates, to ask questions about their impairments and their challenges growing up. David and I played pool and table hockey with a couple of Aussies, a high jumper with half an arm missing and someone with cerebral palsy. I organised a massage for us both. It was a great afternoon. I'm getting back on top of things.

12/9/16 Monday

Because the Village is equipped with fantastic medical equipment, the doctor and physio agreed for me to have an MRI scan to see what caused the loss of feeling in my hand in Montichiari, and the long-term effect from the crash I had before London. It was early in the morning and I sat very still in a machine with ear-piecing noises. From there I just made our training ride at 9.30, with the whole team along the time trial course.

Later I had a 90-minute appointment with Dr Geoff Verrall. He looked at scans, explained to me why I was losing feeling, and inspected the recovery of other injuries. I was blown away at the severity of the injuries, and also shocked when he said I was lucky that I didn't damage the spinal nerve. I was shocked to see two badly crushed vertebrae on the scans. The loss of feeling is from a bulging disk pressing on the nerve, maybe resulting from the most recent crash. But it's not serious and can be managed with exercise. I learnt just how lucky I was but it increased my nervousness about the coming road race because I now have a heightened fear of falling. It couldn't have come at a worse time as I have the road time trial and road race in a couple of days. I discussed with him my changing eye condition and my fear of my world changing and literally shrinking. I told the doc I wasn't ready for this and probably living in a state of denial, but he said that I had crammed so much in already and had excelled with the challenges. I walked out feeling vulnerable, but comforted. I hold him in such high regard; just being around him makes me feel good. I made him a tatted dragonfly in appreciation of his time and support.

13/9/16 Tuesday

Today was a hot 33°. From 9.30 till 11 am we looked again at the time trial course, but this time the roads were closed off. We looked at the starting ramp and had a few efforts. I wasn't keen to do too much. David got frustrated that I was doing so much filming off the back of the tandem, upsetting the balance of the bike. I waited an hour for a haircut and filmed a time-lapse sequence along the flags area; it sort of worked.

14/9/16 Wednesday

Time trial

Not a lot of thought went into the preparation for the time trial apart from the warm up on the ergo and getting into our skin suits, gloves and helmets – and, of course, the last-minute toilet stop. We were calm, focused but not nervous.

Kieran and David had primarily trained for the pursuit event, so the Men's Time Trial B over 30 km was not going to suit their skill set. To make matters worse the event was timed to start at 1:30 pm on a hot and humid Rio day ... and Kieran and David were seeded to ride off seventh (out of 23 contestants). Riders are flagged off at one-minute intervals and it helps to be in the latter part of the draw so you know what time you need to beat ... and have a psychological lift from passing others along the circuit. In their favour was the relative flatness of the course, which suited their heavier body weights.

Dutchmen Stephen de Vries and Patrick Bos were first off the starting ramp and again set a cracking pace. Averaging 50.169 kph over the journey, their time of 35:52.73 was the one to beat and the following five combinations didn't threaten this mark.

Kieran and David were next ...

14/9/16 Wednesday *(continued)*
I enjoyed rolling up to the start of the ramp right on the beach front and looking out over the crowds, but we set off with concerned minds; time trials are far from our favourite event. To hold one pace is taxing and in most cases you look for respite, often sitting behind a bike already out on the course. But in this case it was all about us against the elements, a tail wind out and a strong head wind back. The bike felt good and the sound of the disc wheel whirring made me go harder. David periodically called out the speed, 55, and then we pushed a little harder – 57 through to 60. I knew I was getting a little ahead of myself. I was breathing rapidly and we had only covered 7 km of the 30 km course. Could I hold this pace? David was still pumping those pedals and if we were to have any chance of finishing this race well, I had to get into a rhythm. David called out 'German team ahead' and it spurred me on again. We passed the slower teams convincingly, but all the while we knew that the faster bikes were behind us, chasing us down. The hairpin turn was tight, with a cobblestone path run-off, which David used to execute the turn. We accelerated, bumping over the cobblestone and getting back onto the smooth part of the road. The 7 km head-wind stretch was brutal, but the speed

remained high at 55 kph. David called out as we approached other bikes, but I knew I was in trouble. How would I manage the next lap? My breathing was now erratic, but David stamped out the tempo and I couldn't let him down. On the last lap we dropped the pace to 55 and I was able to find my rhythm again, but in the last 10 km, with a head wind, my stomach was churning and I could feel the power draining from my legs. So I focused on pushing harder. Suddenly my legs were shutting down and I could feel the speed wash away. I knew David was in the same boat; his rocking body indicated he was tiring fast as well. It was a matter of getting to the finish line before we lost too much speed. David was yelling, 'Come on!' and whether it was for him or me I didn't care, I searched for more. On the last two hairpin corners, 2 km and 200 m out from the finish, I dug as deep as I could. But it came with a price. As we crossed the line I turned my head enough so as not vomit down his back. Later I said, 'That makes us even.' There have been a number of times when he has coughed, spat or blown his nose, and I've grimaced, knowing I might cop some of it.

We stopped 100 m after the finish line and didn't move. Our team manager rushed over and gave us water and a towel. I was too exhausted to move, talk or even look up. David was clearly feeling the same. When we finally walked off the course, we had no thought of our place. Someone commented that we were sitting in second but it meant nothing as the faster bikes were yet to finish. As we sat in our little tent a comment was thrown around that we had finished third. 'Don't do that to us,' David said, with a hint of agitation. I shrugged it off as a joke. Even when they showed us the results on the computer it didn't sink in. With such a high quality field it couldn't be possible. Had we really won a bronze medal for Australia?

When we stood on the podium, anyone would have thought we had won the gold, we were so happy. The dark cloud that had been hovering over our heads over the last couple of days had suddenly vanished. Nick and Matt placed 13th, no doubt disappointed with their result.

Kieran and David were not to know this at the time, but at the halfway point they were 23 seconds inside de Vries's time. Finishing on well, they set a time of 35:09.06, 44 seconds better than de Vries and averaging 51.208 kph.

Mostly unaware of what was happening on the circuit, Kieran and David recovered in their tent while we all held our breath and waited to see what times the following 16 riders would record. The Spanish champions came through and still Kieran and David held the gold-medal position. Oz Tandem followed and were nearly two minutes behind. Would Dutchman Vincent ter Shure again be able to knock the Aussies off their top position?

At the half way point ter Shure was 10 seconds in front of Kieran's time and went on to take the lead with an overall time of 34:44.16.

The Netherlands and Australia watched as all other riders failed to beat their potential medal-winning positions and waited for the British champions, Steve Bate and Adam Duggleby to finish. When news came through that at the halfway split the Englishmen were already 11 seconds in front of ter Shure, it was no surprise that they maintained this margin to win gold in 34:35.33.

David laughed off the vomiting experience later when asked how he felt about winning bronze. He told the media that it was worth it to experience the podium:

> We came in as reigning World Champions in the pursuit so we had high expectations, but after that expectation dropped

> I lost all hope (of a medal). I can't describe it, such a relief, an amazing feeling to get something back for the effort, all the work we've put in and all the work in the background by so many people. That is what this is for.

14/9/16 Wednesday *(continued)*

I am still shocked at the speed we averaged, over 50 kph for 30 km – unheard of for me. The event is just running over and over in my head and David and I are feeding off each other's enthusiasm and excitement. The bronze has redeemed everything that we've been working for. Our bike was just a road bike, not a super-duper bike set up for time trials. Clip on bars for David. Normal road bars on the back. No elbow pads for me. The geometry on a proper time trial bike is slightly different. You are further over the bottom brackets and being more bent over makes you more aerodynamic. We didn't have that! It wasn't our event. So it came down to physical ability ... and we just did it!

David's reaction is understandably similar:

> I was very relaxed about the race because I thought that we didn't have much of a chance to medal. I kept thinking that it was hard and that at some point we would be passed. At times I thought we might be racing for a medal ... but then I would say to myself, 'Don't be silly!' I was basically racing for Kieran, for the fun of it and because intrinsically I am competitive.
>
> I told everyone back home to stay up late to watch the pursuit, but not the time trial. I thought it would be a non-event for us. I had decided not to ever wear the podium jacket, unless I deserved it by climbing on to that dais. It's a hefty sized medal and it's beautiful.

15/9/16 Thursday

No riding today, instead I organised to get out of the Village, not just for me but for David. We decided to visit the sailing event because it was so far away and a long bus trip would be good. From there we were able to catch a taxi and go up to Sugarloaf Mountain, overlooking the sailing on the bay, and so we watched the races from the top.

The final event for Kieran and David and the Australian para-cycling team was the 99 km men's tandem road race.

17 /9/16 Saturday

Our race started at 1.30. We rode down about an hour before using the ride as a warm up. It was warm anyway, about 30°C, and the race was three laps of the time trial course (30 km) and the rest in the hills. During the first lap we were called back to the start line, the race cancelled because the ambulance hadn't been present in the follow vehicles. I could see the frustration on the faces of the other riders and disbelief at the lack of organisation. We rolled up to the start finish line for a second time with a field of 23 tandems, all looking edgy and pushing to the front.

Not wanting to miss the opportunity I asked David to attach his tiny action camera to the bike, which is prohibited unless authorised. Reluctantly he agreed, and I nervously watched the officials walking around – I was more nervous about the camera than the race itself.

With the second start, riders surged to the front amid a heightened level of urgency. David positioned us down near the back and didn't do any work on the front. We tried pushing forward up the pack when arriving at the hairpin corners, because riders at the back find themselves working hard to accelerate to get back on the pack. We stayed on the rear of another wheel, saving our legs especially in the head wind. The hills were tough. In each lap we had to ride up two sharp 50 m pinch climbs, a brutal 1 km climb with a gradient of 18%, and another long 3 km 7% gradient climb.

The group broke up on the nasty steep climbs and reformed on the descents. The combined weight of David, me and the bike is about 200 kg, one of the heaviest, and we found ourselves really struggling on the 1 km climb. To our surprise many of the other tandems were struggling too. We were even pulling away ever so slightly, chasing two bikes 25 m ahead. To prevent overheating David would release the brakes coming out of the corner and the bike would immediately accelerate as if it was a motorbike. With a sigh of relief we reached the bottom and went straight into time trial mode to chase the two tandems, now 200 m up the road. The riders behind were chasing us and finally five bikes formed a lead group. Going into the second lap I thought all I had to do was the same as before, but the climbs became more difficult and again the group splintered, with us chasing again. Finally an attack was made by the Dutch and Spanish up the last 3 km climb, dropping Great Britain, the second Spanish team and us. We spent the last 20 km chasing them to the line. We closed the gap between us and third and fourth to 100 m, but our legs were cramping, there was next to no power there. We can't be disappointed. We did everything we could and we were very happy with our efforts to be so close.

Kieran and David were only 42 seconds off the gold medal time of Dutch pair Vincent ter Schure (pilot Timo Fransen) and the second-place Spanish pair of Ignacio Avila Rodriguez (pilot Joan Font Bertoli), and only 12 seconds behind Britain's Steve Bate and Adam Duggleby who rounded out the podium. Oz Tandem came in 13th place, 15 minutes adrift of the winners.

The road race presented another opportunity and with low expectations we rode from the heart, we rode for each other, we rode because we had spent months and months training. We were not racing for a medal, all we wanted was to be able to finish and say, 'Yes we're happy with that ride because we put everything into it.' Dave did a brilliant job reading the race and we lost most of our ground on the descents. Oz Tandem had a terrible campaign. They put a lot of pressure on themselves to win a medal. In comparison, the pressure put on us came from others, people who knew my reputation and expected that having won the last three golds in the pursuit event, I would win again.

This was one of the most difficult campaigns I've experienced, a Games where winning a bronze felt like a gold. I am prouder of this medal because of the journey taken to win it. These Games gave me a taste of the depths of defeat, an experience many athletes have gone through. My focus now wasn't on winning, it was on composure, of being able to hold our heads up and be proud – hard to do when you haven't performed your best.

It's the unexpected things that give us the most joy.

The cycling contingent left Rio with 13 medals. Australia had hit its target of a top five finish with 81 medals, and with half of the 178-strong team first-timers, there was optimism for the 2020 Tokyo campaign.

I chatted to Kieran extensively about where he sees his future in para-cycling. He is the present world champion and still the best Australian male para-cyclist in his classification. The British have taken the lead in both training techniques and cycle technology and their able-bodied and para-cyclists train together. They swap around riders *to gain advantage. The British Olympic cycling team received £30.2 million from UK Sport with the bulk of that money spent on the track, where the variables can be controlled and where most of the medals are on offer. In comparison, the Australian Institute of Sport awarded its cyclists just AU$34.1 million (£18.6 m) for the current four-year Olympic cycle.*

In August 2016, British Cycling's head coach Iain Dyer told the media:

> We've got a really great team of people doing a fantastic job and who will go to the ends of the earth looking for that final marginal gain. It's all about marginal gains, isn't it? That's what we have become famous for. The low-hanging fruit disappeared years ago. There was a lot of talk of people catching up, because they just saw the gains that we had started to make was stuff they could emulate. Now the devil is in the detail. The marginal gains have never been more marginal and aggregating that has never been more important.

These marginal gains include a Manchester velodrome equipped with a series of cameras installed in the ceiling and walls that give coaches accurate data on speed, position on the track and technique. High frequency sound waves are used to clean the bike's chain. Frames are painted with a special resin, similar to that used in Formula One motor racing to improve the aerodynamics. The British have been wearing top-secret Adidas skinsuits and even their cyclists' socks are aerodynamic. There are teams of nutritionists, psychiatrists, psychologists, physiologists, bio-mechanists, performance analysts, physicians, engineers ... and coaches, often recruited from overseas. When the USA unveiled a bike with the crank arm and chain on the left side and claimed it gave them an advantage, British Cycling refuted this because they had already tried it!

The British have mastered a technique called 'periodised training', where the training year is divided and organised to ensure that peak performance is achieved at the optimum time. For the British this is the Olympic Games. A multi-year program involves a gradual increase in training intensity through the pre-competition period, followed by a reduction (tapering) of training, as the competition period draws near.

When following a multi-year periodisation plan, such as the four-year Olympic cycle, the final year is the most important one. That's when the amount of training (the distance covered or time spent) is reduced to prevent injury and fatigue, while the intensity of the workouts is increased to ensure athletes are in top form for the big event. Kieran and David could well have done with more of this and less of the crashes and exhaustion.

Maybe the main advantage of this British thrust is psychological. They have great self-belief and enormous confidence. They know they are the best trained and best equipped – everyone knows it – and this is intimidating.

Long-time Australian high performance boss Kevin Tabotta resigned after Australia's underwhelming Rio campaign to take up a position with World Tour team Orica-Scott, and Cycling Australia has raided British Cycling and Team Sky by luring one of its top coaching and sports science brains, Simon Jones, to lead its rebuild towards the 2020 Tokyo Olympics.

I sought the opinion of Kieran's long-time coach and friend Kevin McIntosh:

> Kieran is the most amazing athlete I've ever come across. I've coached dual Olympic gold medallists, junior world champions, world champions, the whole lot, and I've said this many times ... if God stood before me and said, 'I can give you any one of ability to coach' I would ask for Kieran Modra. He is

> an anomaly, one of the most amazing athletes I've come across. He's pig-headed and he's obstinate, but I don't think I've had more respect for any athlete, or trained any athlete with more ability. Forty-five years of age is not a problem. Not for Kieran. He is so passionate about his cycling. He can do anything when he puts his mind to it. If you take the competition out of Kieran, I don't think you've got Kieran. Even now, if he trained the way he should train and took on board aspects of his physiology, his strengths and weaknesses, he would still be in gold medal winning position. Kieran possesses great strength. He is probably the most powerful athlete I know. His ability to produce power and speed is something he will maintain for years to come. If he's not comfortable with his safety or is losing trust in his equipment, then the answer might be there. Kieran does break things and the equipment needs to be constantly upgraded and changed to suit him. We have the technology, we just need to do it better. I've always respected and liked him for who he is. He's not only an amazing athlete, but an amazing person and in spite of his disability, he uses every aspect of his abilities to enjoy life. Kieran is revered around the world for being an athlete.

World records in tandem pursuit were smashed in Rio and for Kieran to reach them, he feels there would have to be a massive injection of funding and he would need to train as a full-time athlete; more in line with what the able-bods are doing, which is even more structured. This would take him away from family for longer periods.

I feel fortunate to be able to still mix it with the new age athletes with so much ability. The reality of retirement is almost certain. Even though the sport has become a huge part of my life, I feel I need to let go. Not because I'm not good enough (in some cases I want to go again to prove I can ride at world record pace), but for my family. I want to spend more time with them and focus on their pursuits rather than mine. To me cycling is still a hobby. I don't get paid a full-time wage like many of my international competitors, and so I feel I can't keep pouring in more and more time and watch my family suffer. It is hard to learn that many of my competitors get a good wage to do their sport and maybe that's why their times are as fast as the able-bodied athletes. I am very grateful for the support I have received from Australia, but can't help but think how good it would be in those athlete's shoes.

To some I am an inspiration and a motivational force, but to my family I'm just Dad. So much has been put on hold – finances, time with my girls and time with my wife. I've been in and out of work due to sport and now see the importance of securing a steady income. I've spent over half my life competing in international sport and facing life without it is daunting; I feel a little lost. That is probably why I've retired and come back again and again. Now I want to make it stick.

But I haven't been to Japan yet. I wonder what it's like?

Acknowledgements

I have always wanted to write a book, so huge thanks go to Kieran, Kerry, Holly, Makala and Janae for letting me into your lives and so generously sharing your experiences with me ... and always with a smile.

Thanks as well to Kieran's family – Theo and Sylvia, Darren and Tammy, Mark and Tamara and Tania and Simon. During the writing of this book we all experienced the highs and lows of family life. Darren contributed to this book and I hope that he is pleased with the outcome. He is a man of God and with his Saviour now. Someday we will all be together.

Many helped with editing the manuscript: my wife Marley, Sylvia Modra, Jan Wallent, Erica Vaughan, Jenny Patching, and Sonia and Erich Holzknecht. Thank you for your suggestions and encouragement.

Thanks to the many people I interviewed, people important in Kieran and Kerry's lives: Peggy Bell, John Hamann, Dennis Peck, Ann Baillie, Jenny Flood, Kevin McIntosh, Nick Dean, David Baker, Dr Harold Handley and Maria Smith – and I apologise to any others I may have overlooked. Thank you for sharing so fully and enthusiastically.

I sincerely appreciated Patricia Sumerling's, Leanne Hutton's and Geoff Munzberg's advice on how to go about this: Theo Modra,

John Veage and Colin Gill for most of the photography; and Peter and Erika Kaesler for your cleverness in tandem design.

I needed sponsorship and Rajini Vasan and Eye Play Sport answered the call. Raj, not only have you shown this project wonderful generosity, but so much enthusiasm for our shared goal to give others the opportunity to be inspired by Kieran and his family. Thank you for making this happen.

Thanks to Molly Jureidini at Wakefield Press for first sharing my vision and then Julia Beaven for making this all possible. As you know, Julia, this is my first attempt at writing a book, and I have learned so much from your experience and professionalism.

However, the person who knows the countless hours I've spent authoring is my lovely wife, Marley. Not only has she endured a partner who slipped out of bed and on to a computer at any hour of the night, but she has travelled innumerable kilometres and enthusiastically participated in many of the interviews. She now belongs to a group that knows what it's like to try to communicate with someone who is mentally miles away composing the next line in a manuscript. Thanks, Marley, for your support, patience and love.

Wakefield Press is an independent publishing and distribution company based in Adelaide, South Australia. We love good stories and publish beautiful books. To see our full range of books, please visit our website at wakefieldpress.com.au where all titles are available for purchase. To keep up with our latest releases, news and events, subscribe to our monthly newsletter.

Find us!

Facebook: facebook.com/wakefield.press
Twitter: twitter.com/wakefieldpress
Instagram: instagram.com/wakefieldpress

Printed in Australia
AUHW011228151119
320050AU00004B/5

9 781743 056998